153.47

FEB -- 2003

J U D Y   F

T0659366

getting Over getting Mad

Positive Ways to
Manage Anger
in Your Most Important Relationships

DISCARD

Forbush Memorial Library
118 MAIN STREET P.O. BOX 468
WESTMINSTER, MA 01473-0468

CONARI PRESS
Berkeley, California

Copyright © 2001 by Judy Ford

All Rights Reserved. No part of this book may be used or reproduced in any manner whatsoever without written permission, except in the case of brief quotations in critical articles or reviews. For information, contact: Conari Press, 2550 Ninth Street, Suite 101, Berkeley, California 94710-2551.

Conari Press books are distributed by Publishers Group West.

ISBN: 1-57324-555-0

Cover Photography: Images copyright © 1998 and 1999 PhotoDisc, Inc.
Cover Design: Suzanne Albertson
Book Design: Ingrid Owen
Author Photo: Amanda Ford

Library of Congress Cataloging-in-Publication Data

Ford, Judy, 1944–
    Getting over getting mad : positive ways to manage anger in your
 most important relationships / Judy Ford.
        p.   cm.
    Includes bibliographical references.
    ISBN 1-57324-555-0
    1. Anger. 2. Interpersonal relations. I. Title.
BF575.A5 F67 2001
152.4'7—dc21   00-011713

Printed in the United States of America on recycled paper.

01 02 03   Data   10 9 8 7 6 5 4 3 2 1

A Native American elder once described his own inner struggles in this manner: "Inside of me there are two dogs. One of the dogs is mean and evil. The other dog is good. The mean dog fights the good dog all the time." When asked which dog wins, he reflected for a moment and replied, "The one I feed the most."

—UNKNOWN

GETTING OVER GETTING MAD

PART 4 In the Presence of Colleagues   145

"Only Dogs Get Mad"

My grandmother was an old-fashioned grandma. She wore her white hair twisted into two buns, one behind each ear. She was known for her fabulous flower garden, and she made the best graham cracker frosting sandwiches I ever ate. She was a wonderful grandma, but she had an annoying habit that drove my family nuts. Whenever anyone within hearing distance got angry or even slightly annoyed, Grandma would pipe up and recite, over and over, "Only dogs get mad! . . . Only dogs get mad!" You see, Grandma thought that people should not get angry—especially not people in her family. Just feeling angry was a terrible thing. If my brother Jerry, my sister Kathy, or I were in a tiff, as siblings often are, there she'd be, cautioning us in a high-pitched, sing-song voice, "Only dogs get mad!"—which, of course, made us even madder.

Grandma's refrain extended to everyone—my mother, my father, my aunts and uncles. We would try our best to ignore her, but she would chant the phrase loudly enough that we would be compelled to stop our discussion, look at each other, and roll our eyes. This made Grandma especially pleased with herself, believing she had indeed saved us from the terrible sin of getting mad. But we felt worse. Yes, we had stopped our fighting, usually going our separate ways, but nothing was resolved and there was an uneasy distance between us. We were left alone to sort out what had happened. Grandma was happy, but we were confused. I learned only later, after years of being told, "Only dogs get mad," that I felt guilty whenever I felt angry.

My whole family adopted a policy of "squelching anger." In psychological terms, the defense mechanisms of "suppression," "repression," and "denial" were in full swing. Fighting, disagreeing, arguing, quarreling, clashing, and even mild squabbling were sinful and to be avoided. We had conflicts and differences of opinion, for sure, but we kept them to ourselves. We felt ashamed of ourselves for disagreeing and embarrassed about getting annoyed. We were afraid to express ourselves freely. We were clueless about relating to one another, because we had no tools for resolving the natural conflicts that arise within a family. We were left with migraine headaches, scowls on our faces, and, worst of all, no ability to get close to one another or to know each other well.

Almost all families have similar difficulties. In twenty-five years of counseling families, I've seen how suppressing anger leads to hard feelings and bitterness and ultimately to increased upset, walls of resentment, and long-standing grudges. The inability to express natural anger leads to a growing discontentment with life. Even more detrimental to family life and healthy relationships is unacknowledged anger that comes out in distorted ways. Sarcasm, manipulation, passive-aggressive acts, physical illness, depression, rebellion, and violence all result from the inability to express anger and resolve disputes. Distorted anger damages relationships between husbands and wives, parents and children, friends, colleagues at work.

Even at a young age, my grandmother's saying—"Only dogs get mad"—didn't make sense to me. I've heard accounts of rabid dogs attacking people, but I've never actually seen a mad dog myself. Many dogs, if taunted or teased, will walk away. Others are more feisty and may growl, snarl, or snap to let you know that you've gone too far, but seldom does a dog get so agitated that it will lash out and hurt someone. If you respect dogs, they respect you, and you can live peacefully and joyfully together. Though very few of us have been witness to a mad dog attack, almost all of us have seen or experienced the fallout of a mad person in a frenzy. Perhaps, like me, you've heard mad people yelling obscenities from their cars. Perhaps you know adults who are so filled with rage that they've forgotten how to respond responsibly to the present moment or to walk away. You've read newspaper accounts of children so angry they take guns to school and shoot up their classrooms. Far too many people—adults and children—don't know how to communicate their frustrations effectively. They scream, rant, rave, and blame others for what's wrong in their own lives. They inflict harm on others and violence on themselves. We have all known or heard about a person who was so angry that she went on a rampage. Others literally go mad and have to be locked up.

Aside from escalating violence, the effects of unresolved anger can rule our daily lives. The courts are backed up with people who can't resolve their own disputes. Children are tormented by bullies, coworkers spread rumors about each other, couples separate and don't speak to each other. Divorced parents fight over their children. People bemoan the fact that manners and good sportsmanship seem to be things of the past. When folks work at jobs they don't like, buy things they don't need, and try to compete with their neighbors, everyday life becomes a mad frenzy.

Getting Over Getting Mad aims to help you recognize anger within yourself and toward the important people in your life before the anger turns into a permanent state of madness. By recognizing anger, you can take steps to express yourself clearly rather than dumping on another person. Instead of carrying around a gunnysack of outdated grudges, you can be rid of the unnecessary burden. Your relationships will go more smoothly. You'll be able to clear the air, so that your contacts with other people are full of tenderness instead of strain and tension. With the tools presented in *Getting Over Getting Mad*, you can relax when your children are arguing, and you can teach them how to resolve their disagreements. When your husband says nothing is wrong but is slamming doors in frustration, when your wife is sarcastic, when your child is having a fit, when your coworker is demanding that you do it her way, *Getting Over Getting Mad* will show you how to address the underlying issues before irrationality and madness take over.

My hope is that *Getting Over Getting Mad* will inspire you to resolve your conflicts peacefully, so that you can fully enjoy your relationships. By taking responsibility for your anger, you can clear the way for sweeter connections to the important people in your life. You'll still get mad, because you're human, but you can work through it, get over it, laugh about it, and move on.

I HAVE PLENTY TO BE MAD ABOUT—AND SO DO YOU!

"I'm going to write a book about love," I told William. "Love, love, love," he said half-mockingly. "Haven't you written enough about love? Write me a book about anger," he said. "Now that would interest me!"

I could understand why he'd be interested in the subject. During the previous seven months he'd completed several rounds of chemo and radiation treatments and been told by his oncologist that there was nothing more to do. He could barely walk from the bed to the bathroom, his breathing was labored, and the hospice chaplain and a team of nurses were visiting daily. William had non-Hodgkin's lymphoma, and I didn't have to ask to know that my best friend, helpmate, and loving companion of ten years had a few weeks, maybe a month to live. He had every reason to be angry.

And I had my own reasons to be mad. Twenty years earlier, Jack, the man of my dreams, my boyfriend for five years, my husband for six years, had died suddenly of a heart attack. He died in March, exactly one month after we both turned twenty-nine. I wasn't prepared; how could I have been? I grew up believing that if you respected your parents, went to church, worked hard, and were nice to other people, you'd live happily ever after. When it didn't turn out that way, I didn't like it. Months of shock turned to years of mourning, and slowly became desperation. Thoughts of "Why?" tortured me night and day. "Help me!" I cried out to the universe. But God didn't hear me, or didn't answer. Or I didn't listen or know how to listen. Perhaps God did answer and I didn't understand. I wasn't sure.

Was there a God? I was lonely, afraid, hurt, sad, grieving, and angry, plagued by many questions.

Now William was dying and I was losing another partner. I didn't like this either. "Why do I have to go through life alone? Why do I feel mad? Is it OK to be angry at God?" These were important questions; asking them brought up more questions and then slowly some answers—many of which I share in these pages.

This book has been on the back burner for the seven years since William died. I wrote the *Wonderful Ways to Love* series—the books that I had told William I wanted to write—and while involved in that process I observed how anger affects relationships. In my work as a family counselor, I've counseled and spoken with thousands of people, and I've learned firsthand that we all have circumstances—from something as major as the death of a family member, divorce, or illness, to minor irritants like fender benders, spilled milk, overdrawn checking accounts, rejection, and disappointments—that stimulate our anger. The reasons for our anger are varied, but if we're alive and walking around, something is bound to trigger an angry response. How we deal with anger is reflected in our relationships and families and is a significant factor in determining whether or not we work out our differences. It influences the quality of our relationships and how fulfilled and peaceful we are. My clients and the people who attended my workshops have given me permission to share their stories in this book. Their names have been changed and their circumstances disguised, but their struggles and the victories remain. By facing their anger and dealing with their frustration, they were able to love more fully.

While I know that we all have reasons to be angry, I can't think of one good reason to stay mad for very long. Life isn't easy; it seldom goes according to plan. Some folks get angry, get over it, and move on. Others stay mad for so long that it sours their dispositions, pollutes their daily living, and corrupts their connections. Some folks take the difficulty in life and turn it into something better—they become more loving, more radiant, and sweeter. They become positive beacons of hope. Others become enveloped in bottomless hate and bitterness. They become agents of destruction. No matter what injustice comes to me, I don't want to be like that. Do you? I want to use my situation to help me grow, so that I can enjoy my life. I will get angry, but I won't stay mad.

During the months that William was ill, we both got angry, but since we knew our time together was limited we decided not to waste precious moments staying mad. When he snapped at me because I accidentally dropped the oxygen, or when I was cranky with him because I'd been up all night, we argued quickly, solved the problem as best we could, and moved on.

Life with our loved ones is very short, and if you want to enjoy each moment, it's best if you can express your anger gently and move on. To enjoy the sweetness of being connected, you have to know the difference between distorted anger, which tears families apart, and healthy anger, which keeps relationships thriving. We can get angry with the people we love, they can get deeply annoyed with us, and through it all, we can work it out together and come to a place of understanding, acceptance, and joy.

PART 1 In the Presence of Yourself

What can we gain by sailing to the moon if we are not able to cross the abyss that separates us from ourselves? This is the most important of all voyages of discovery, and without it, all the rest are not only useless, but disastrous.

—THOMAS MERTON

Anger is the abyss that separates us from ourselves. From losing our tempers easily to feeling a slow burn to hiding how irritated we really feel, all of us experience anger as a troubling emotion. We all have trouble identifying anger when we feel it and difficulty expressing it appropriately once it's felt. When we're depressed and filled with panic, we blame it on our circumstances, our jobs, our hormones, the traffic, and each other. When we're gnarly to our loved ones and rude to complete strangers, we feel perfectly justified. It's their fault! A myriad of things make us mad, and we have a million excuses for our behavior.

How we express anger depends on our circumstances and conditioning. We hide under pleasant public faces, then in private we rant and rave, threaten, hit, smash objects, and throw things. Men and women are equally capable of verbally abusing each other. And we've all known folks who dump their anger onto children or onto someone less powerful than themselves. When it comes to anger, everyone's halo is tarnished.

Anger causes tremendous confusion. That's because there are

two sides of anger. On the one side, anger is an indispensable emotion, which when used productively allows us to develop ourselves and our relationships. On the other side, when anger covers up pain and fear, it clogs our energy, dilutes our joy, and keeps us off track, going in circles, making no headway. Instead of helping us, anger becomes self-defeating.

The moment you identify anger and admit to yourself that you feel it, you've taken a giant leap toward freeing yourself from its clenches. You experience a moment of liberation when you acknowledge that you're not happy about something, and even though you may not yet know what to do about it, you're not going to pretend any longer that everything is perfect. In that breakthrough moment, you're released from the fog of denial and can tap into the energy that you'll need to move your life along.

Often a spiritual or personal crisis provokes this shift. When your psyche is cracked, when your heart is broken, when the world you've built your dreams upon is lying in shambles, there's not much left to do except to notice miracles and patterns. Miracles are brief "hellos" from the Divine that assure you of a better way, that a bigger plan is in the making. Patterns are automatic behaviors that you've overlearned. In the past, those behaviors may have helped you survive, but they've now outlived their usefulness. Seeing and changing your patterns requires your attention and your willingness to struggle. Like it or not, we all go through life's initiations, and in the process we discover who we really are. Often that might include asking the questions: "Who am I? Where am I going? What am I doing? Why am I feeling so mad?"

Getting to know yourself and all your emotions—including anger—is the process of becoming an individual. It is not a quick or an easy trek. It's certainly not as simple as deciding one night that you won't lash out again and then putting your resolve into practice. It's a process full of thrashing around. No one gets it right all the time. It takes years of polishing and practicing.

It's worth the difficulty, however, because when you're honest with yourself you do feel better, and life gets sweeter. So try not to beat yourself up for what you did or didn't do in the past. Instead, notice how your circumstances are changing and what you're learning. Say to yourself: I can get angry, but I won't stay mad.

Frown Freely

When you're mad, hurt, or afraid, frown and frown freely for as long as you like. It sounds simplistic to say that frowning can be the beginning of a change in some of your destructive patterns, but it's worked for me. Frowning actually makes me feel better than pasting on a phony-baloney grin. Here's my experience:

> I was raised in the "Be nice" school of anger management, which holds that no matter what I'm feeling or thinking I should always put on a happy face. I can still hear my mother's voice saying, "Why can't you just be nice?" After my husband died, I thought that I literally had to "grin and bear it." Believe me, I was trying my best to smile, but I couldn't fake it. I couldn't laugh, giggle, or pretend that I was fine. I was frowning and gloomy most of the time. People noticed and didn't like it. Strangers made the most ridiculous statements to me." It can't be all that bad," they said. "Smile," they coaxed. Wanting to be nice, I'd try to accommodate them, but wearing a mask of cheerfulness felt so bizarre that I could barely muster up a grimace. I was frowning and struggling to ignore the disapproving glances.
>
> Standing in the grocery line, the clerk said, "Smile, it's not that bad." Without skipping a beat or apologizing I stunned myself by answering, "I don't feel like smiling. My husband died."
>
> The clerk's eyes widened and he stuttered something about being sorry and not wanting to upset me. His face turned red and he bagged the groceries as quickly as he could. I told him not to worry, but I must admit I felt relieved to see him blush and grateful that I hadn't apologized.

Whatever you do, please don't paste a phony smile on your face. Plastic smiles do damage to your soul. We've all known people who've wore silly grins while they talked about something sad. This tendency to smile even when you don't feel like it developed in childhood, when our parents coaxed us into smiling for the camera or for other people even though we didn't feel like it. Making kids smile when they aren't up to it sends a message that it's not OK to be authentic. Even in front of the camera it's better to capture genuine irritable faces than phony stares. The most fascinating snapshots are candid, those that catch people being real. Fake people plaster on smiles when they'd rather be crying, or they smile when they're angry or sad. Slowly they lose touch with their souls.

Some of the most interesting characters are slightly cantankerous. You wouldn't think of telling grumpy old men to smile. People like Walter Matthau or Albert Einstein aren't smiling for the camera. Sophia on *The Golden Girls* is charmingly cute, cranky, and candid. The next time you see a frown on someone's face, don't be so quick to judge them. Perhaps they're simply hurt or angry. Be happy that they can show it, and that they're being honest.

 Frowning when you are unhappy is healthier than covering up your pain by smiling.

Uncover the Hurt

Underneath each little sting of anger is a hurt, a disappointment, a letdown, a small betrayal. Don, a client of mine, says, "When I'm hurt, I get angry. Instead of feeling sad, I get mad. I act as if I don't care. I don't want anyone to know what bothers me." Anger and hurt swirl around together. Anger acts as a shield, covering the hurt underneath. Sometimes we pay more attention to the anger and over-look the wound. If you ignore how hurt you feel, anger is guaranteed to surface unexpectedly. Figuring out what the pain is about will automatically lessen the anger.

Carla wants her marriage to survive, but she can no longer toler-ate Don's irresponsibility. Don is unable to hold a job, because when-ever he gets annoyed he tells the boss where to go and walks out the door. He makes commitments but doesn't follow through on them.

Don's father abandoned his family when Don was thirteen years old. His mother was devastated and turned to Don for support. Don tried to please his mother, but she was never satisfied. If Don mowed the lawn, washed the car, did the dishes, or folded the laundry, it never quite met her standards. The more she criticized, the more dis-couraged Don became and the more hurt he felt. He didn't argue about the chores; he just wouldn't complete his homework. The look on his face said something was wrong, but if anyone asked, he shrugged his shoulders.

Instead of crying, Don kept his pain locked away. Once in awhile something unexpected would poke a hole in the wall that he'd encased himself in; then he'd explode. Afterward he would feel ashamed and scold himself for being a failure. He was depressed and immobilized.

You may not know that you're covering up hurt with anger, but if you're troubled, worried, anxious, pacing the floor, depressed, out of sorts, snapping, raging, bellyaching, and going nowhere fast, chances are good that something is gnawing at you. If people describe you as negative, if they have to walk on eggshells around you, or if you'd describe yourself as a "people pleaser," you've prob-ably been avoiding pain.

When feeling out of sorts, try to see all the details of what hap-pened. Perhaps somebody insulted you. Perhaps a memory of old rejection, or a wound from the past needs healing. Perhaps you're feeling left out. Close your eyes and review the situation. Run the scene in your mind and lean into the pain as it arises. Let it hurt like hell, cry, scream, pound your fists. Go into it, don't avoid it. Accept it and experience it. Joy and pain go together—they're both part of life. If you numb yourself to pain, you will also be numb to joy.

 Anger is like armor—we put it on to protect ourselves from pain. It never works, because the ache is underneath.

Give Yourself Permission to Be Human

You're upset, you feel a rush of adrenaline, and you say to yourself, "To hell with it!," but you know you aren't thinking straight. You don't want to lose your composure, but you do. You're shaking and you can't remember anything good about the person who ten minutes earlier was the love of your life. Well, you're human.

All human beings get angry. We get mad, blow up, lose our cool, get miffed, throw temper tantrums, get agitated, rant and rave, scream, get pissed off, pout, and sulk. You have, I have, and so have many saints. We've blown up with good reason, and we've been up in arms when we weren't sure why.

Men, women, and children of all ages get angry. Men get angry at women, women get angry at men. Parents lose their patience and snap at their children; children fuss, holler, and throw temper tantrums. Brothers and sisters squabble, lovers quarrel and make up. Husbands and wives have spats, blame each other, defend themselves, apologize, and have the same old argument over again. Coworkers, team members, employers, and employees have differences. It's integral to the human condition.

Brain science offers insight on why we fly off the handle so easily. Everything we see and hear is scanned by the part of the brain called the amygdala. The amygdala—the keeper of emotional memories—sends emergency messages to the rest of the brain and body, ordering instantaneous "fight or flight" when it perceives danger. Unfortunately the amygdala doesn't do the best job of analyzing the information; it often sends an emergency message when there really isn't one.

But brain science doesn't console you when you're shaking. So you try to justify your behavior. Sometimes you're able find good reasons to be mad, and you end up feeling smug. Unfortunately, feeling smug and self-righteous doesn't add much love or affection to your relationships, and if you continue in that habitual pattern, you'll end up more alone then you've ever been. When all is said and done, it's the quality of your relationship with those you love that matters. Are you using anger to improve your relationships, or are you pushing family, friends, and colleagues away?

To remain close to our loved ones, to live joyful lives, we have to manage our anger. We need to keep each other emotionally and physically safe. Our loved ones must be able to trust that even though we're angry, we will not hurt them with our words or actions. They need reassurance that if we are upset, we'll tell them directly. We won't hold it against them or stab them in the back.

 Here's a pledge to make: I'm human, and it's natural to get upset. So that I don't hurt myself or others, I will learn to express my anger constructively.

See Anger as a Blessing

It's a blessing to know when you're angry. My client, Annie, told me about the time she discovered a small blessing in her anger:

> Rachelle walked into the door of our apartment wearing my black short skirt and my favorite blue sweater. I saw her and thought to myself, "Those clothes sure look familiar." Right away she announces, "I borrowed your clothes. I hope that's OK?" I was shocked into numbness at her audacity, but that lasted about two seconds, and before she was out of the hallway, I was boiling. "No, it's not OK! I want you to ask me before you borrow my things." I didn't yell, but she knew that I was unhappy.
>
> I finished eating my lunch and wondered why she thought that it was OK to walk in to my room and take my clothes without checking with me. Later when I saw that she had thrown my clothes on the bed, I was bubbling up again.
>
> I called three people to check out if I was being ridiculous and if my angry feelings were justified. My friends listened to the story, and all of them said they could understand my feelings. That night I wrote Rachelle a letter explaining why her actions bothered me. I told her I didn't want her to borrow anything in my room or bathroom without asking permission. She could use anything in the rest of the apartment, but my room and bathroom were off limits. I taped the letter to her door and I went to bed. I felt better, but I was nervous about what she might say. The next morning she was gone, but she'd left me a note saying that she was sorry and wouldn't do it again. The following day the awkwardness between us was gone.

Annie was angry but she didn't attack. Instead of directing her anger at Rachelle, she took charge of her own emotions. She acknowledged her predicament and gave herself the day to calm down. She thought about what results she wanted to achieve. Annie decided that a sensible approach was needed to enhance her relationship with her roommate.

Annie discovered, as you can too, that it's good to know that you're angry; it's good to talk it over with friends; it's good to handle it quickly, set limits, and clear the air. It's good for you, for your friendships, for love relationships, for families, at work. It's good to know that it's possible for you to get angry and handle it well.

 Anger can be a positive force for change—not for changing others, but for changing yourself.

Be Courageous about Your Imperfections

It's a sign of good mental health when we accept the negative aspects of our personalities. Carl Jung called these negative qualities our "shadow side." If you don't recognize your shadow, it will sneak up on you, cause you harm, haunt you, and eventually destroy you. When you suppress a thought or feeling that exists within you and pretend it isn't there, you relegate it to the basement of your consciousness. Suppressing your shadow side gives it the greatest possible power over you.

The person who denies his angry tendencies operates under the false assumption that by avoiding looking at anger, it will go away. He is only fooling himself. Striving to hide our anger gets us into more trouble, causes more frustration, and sometimes brings about a neurosis where none existed before. The harder you try to hide your inclinations, the more miserable you become. Other people can tell when you're angry, and even though you deny it to yourself, you're not fooling anyone.

Insight is the ability to see what we do without making harsh judgments against ourselves. Insight allows us to understand our actions so that we can choose how to behave next time. It puts us in charge of our behavior, empowers us, and makes us responsible for our feelings and our actions. Examining our angry patterns is the first step to finding another way.

There's great liberation in naming our angry tendencies. Only when we don't admit to something does it have power to control us. Bring it into the light, and its power is greatly reduced. Jill admits that she pouts and gets sarcastic when she's mad. Robert is like a lot of guys: the only emotion he shows is anger. With a little bit of honest self-examination both were able to overcome self-defeating leanings. Here's the exercise they did; you might want to try it. On a sheet of paper, write this sentence five times: "When I get angry, I...."

Now go back and fill in the blanks. Jill wrote, "When I get angry I try to pretend I'm not, say snide things, worry about it for days, get headaches, and get depressed." Robert wrote, "When I get angry I think the worst of people, think nothing will ever work out, slam doors, drink too much, get mean."

Now do as Jill and Robert did, and ask yourself, "Does this behavior suit me?" If pouting works for you, you can certainly keep doing it, but if it doesn't fit you anymore, identifying your tendency frees you to explore what behavior could replace it. Facing the truth—especially the difficult truths about ourselves—is an exhilarating experience and a courageous act. The very decision to know the truth is in itself is an act of self-acceptance. Facing the angry aspects of your personality means you're willing to face your own life, and by doing so you can use anger as a catalyst for something new.

 Acknowledging our own imperfections gives us power over them.

Focus on Your True Nature

If you're worried that feeling or expressing anger means that you're a bad person, here's a Zen story to consider:

> A young student goes to his master and says, "My problem is that I'm angry and I can't seem to do anything about it. Will you help me?"
>
> The master responds, "Show me your anger."
>
> The student objects, saying, "I can't show it to you, because I'm not angry right now."
>
> "Very well," replied the master. "Then the next time that you're angry, bring your anger directly to me."
>
> "Oh, but I can't do that either," the student explains, "because by the time I get to you I won't be angry anymore."
>
> The master nodded and said, "You can't show me your anger and you can't bring your anger to me because anger is not your true nature."

The Zen story raises two of life's big questions: "What is our true nature?" and, "What is my anger?" All the great teachers, from Buddha to Aristotle to Jesus, call us to reflect on these questions and to consider what our deepest nature is, and to discover who we are and how we want to behave.

The great teachers tell us that anger is not our true nature. No matter how angry you are, no matter what angry thoughts you have, no matter what angry acts you've committed, no matter how bitter and resentful you feel, your true nature is not limited by your anger. As a student in the school of life, you're required to complete the course on anger, but your anger is not who you are—you are much, much more.

 Use anger to learn about your true nature—what you want and need and who you really are.

Take Care of Yourself

I'm sure you've noticed that whenever you have a boil, a burn, a toothache, a sliver, a disappointment, or a deep heartache, it draws your attention. Your mind is distracted, and you can't fully concentrate on the task in front of you. The pain is there poking at you, interfering with whatever you'd rather be doing.

It's usually better to get the cavity filled before it starts keeping you up at night, and it's usually advisable to figure out what's troubling you and fix it right away. Ignoring yourself, like ignoring a leaking faucet, eventually causes more trouble.

Many of us learned to take care of others before we care for ourselves. We meet our obligations to others willingly, but are stressed by all the pulls on our attention. Faith, a sixth-grade teacher, mother of two boys, owner of two cats and one dog, wife, and caretaker of her elderly parents, makes sure that the kids are happy, her husband and animals are fed, her parents have been driven to their appointments, the lunches are packed, her phone calls returned, the papers graded, and the house picked up before she allows herself to sit down. On the kitchen wall is a calendar; each day is filled with appointments, after-school activities, and social obligations. Faith wants to squeeze in exercise or an outing with her girlfriends, but seldom finds the time. Her husband, Stan, a contractor with twenty employees, provides very well for his family—a four-bedroom home, a boat, a cabin, vacations, cars, and private schools. He volunteers at church and is on the go from early morning until he falls asleep on the couch at night. He's lucky if he gets to go fishing with his buddies once a year. Stan and Faith haven't taken a vacation alone since their ten-year-old was born. They give great dinner parties, they have a wide circle of friends, but they snap and pick at each other. They don't hold hands anymore.

Faith and Stan are experts at paying attention to what outsiders need, but they're irritable with each other. When Stan is stressed or frustrated, he's critical, puts Faith down, and is sarcastic. Faith's style is different: she doesn't know when she's upset. She smiles and remains pleasant except when she's exhausted; then she sulks and complains. Both feel guilty.

If you're a person who expresses anger destructively, whether by being aggressive or withdrawing, your spouse will react negatively.

When you deny upset, your partner gets a confusing message. They sense that you're upset, but you say you're not. If you're aggressive, others might return the aggression, or they'll ignore you and think, "There he goes again." They'll stop taking you seriously.

You may be asking yourself, "Is it true that paying attention to myself will bring me clarity and resolution?" If you admit to yourself and to someone else, "Yes, I am angry that I have to give another dinner party," or "Yes, I'm angry that I have these financial responsibilities," you'll at the very least feel better for telling the truth. And that is the beginning of finding a solution.

 Taking good care of yourself is the cure for resentment. When you say "No" to outside demands or obligations that you don't want, grudges and bitterness vanish.

Get to Know the Little Devil Within

There's a little devil in all of us. And when that little devil is mad, she's determined to settle the score. A lovely, intelligent women rented a car, disguised herself with a wig, drove to her ex's place, and flattened his car tires. She felt perfectly justified in doing so; in fact she bragged to me about it. Have you ever done something like that? The little devil in us wants revenge. We've been harmed and we demand retribution. When the little devil sees red, he makes sure to have the last word and settle the score.

Healthy boundary-line anger comes and goes quickly unless it's mounted for revenge. All of us have used anger to make a case against someone we didn't like. We've used anger to manipulate, gain power, to get our own way. We've plotted, schemed, and kept the argument going. Then, instead of coming and going, anger settles; instead of overflowing with love and good spirit, hostility takes over. Hostility is the dark side of anger, and it's very dangerous to your spirit.

When someone pokes fun at you, does it make good sense to pitch it back? When your little devil meets her little devil, two wrongs don't make either of you right. When Larry laughed at Joe's cowboy boots, Joe laughed back and said, "I guess my boots are out of style in the city." When Larry continued, Joe firmly said, "You and I disagree on how I should dress."

When others are laughing at you, judging you, making you wrong, instead of getting angry back, you can say, "I see what you mean, and others might agree with you, but this is how I do it." You can hold your ground without being mean; instead of behaving like a demon, you can retain your integrity. Instead of hissing, "You shouldn't say that," you can say, "This is what I think." With these responses your adversary's little devil calms down. When someone humiliates you, try an angelic retort that's gentle yet firm: "We don't agree," or "Maybe you're right," or "Let me think about that," or "I don't see it that way." You can stick up for yourself, you can walk away, you can ignore it, and you can smile.

 The best retort to a put-down is to agree with part of it, ignore the rest of it, and don't take it too seriously.

Move Out of Uproar

It seems that there are chronically angry people everywhere. Doctors, lawyers, politicians, policeman, Web designers, teachers, students, laborers, millionaires, and street people all suffer from the same affliction. You can tell it by the way they snap at the smallest irritation and explode at the tiniest inconvenience. They bubble over with hostility. People are chewing on everything, full of negativity. They act as though life comes with guarantees, and when something doesn't suit them, they sue.

Some people like being mad. It makes them feel powerful and in control. If they stopped being angry they might be sad, in emotional pain, afraid, or full of despair, and since they don't like feeling vulnerable they carry a chip on their shoulder. The most dangerous people are the ones who don't even know that they're angry yet are very hostile. They no longer recognize angry feelings; they live in a permanent state of uproar.

Uproar is a way of making one's own concerns more important than anyone else's. It's the angry person's syndrome. An angry person imagines an insult and immediately hurls insults right back. They overpower others with threats and loud voices.

When my clients who are in permanent state of uproar speak about themselves, practically every other word they use is *should*. "I should do this," or "He should do that." When the messages that you give yourself are filled with "shoulds," you're bound to feel upset. Looking at life from the point of view of "should" will not help you—it will only make you feel angry because you'll so often be disappointed. *Can't* and *have to* are two other thought-forms that cripple us and lead to uproar.

To move out of uproar, it helps if you change what you're thinking and saying. "Possibility thinking" is more relaxing. Change your "It's not possible" into "Maybe it is possible." Change your "I can't" into "I could," or "Maybe I can."

To extricate yourself from uproar you need friends, people whom you can really talk to, who've been there themselves and are ready to share how they have overcome their destructive tendencies. You might find these kinds of friends in a support group or an anger management class. The greatest friend you can have is one who understands your pain and anger but doesn't let you become a permanent victim of it. He pulls you out of the muck, stops your incessant complaining. He tells you the truth and demands the same from you. She asks you to drop hostility and replace it with goodwill. She brings out the best you.

 Notice that *anger* is one letter short of *danger.* A little anger is helpful; too much anger is hurtful.

Learn Spiritual Lessons from Anger

All anger—even the irrational kind—has a significant underlying cause and an important message for you. Just as you can learn many spiritual lessons through love, you can learn powerful spiritual lessons through anger. Knowing yourself is a joy; a large component of knowing yourself involves listening to the deeper messages that come with anger. When you look at yourself from a spiritual vantage point, you'll discover that anger can lead you to gratefulness. It can take you to your soul.

For anger to transform you, however, you must be willing to struggle with existential questions and existential anger. When you face the fundamental reality that life is unfair, you'll confront the inevitably of loss and death. You don't like things to go wrong because it reminds you—at least on an unconscious level—that there are many things in life you can't control. That's why when you get a flat tire you kick the car, when you lock yourself out of the house you throw your wallet, when you break your favorite antique vase you swear. Anger and loss are part of life, as are personal disappointment and family turmoil. Life doesn't go smoothly, things go wrong, you can't control others, you can't control your beloved; eventually you and your loved ones die.

Fortunately that's not the entire story. There is the other side. When you get a flat tire you may feel angry because you'll be late for your appointment, but you can feel grateful that you have a car. When you lock yourself out of the house, you might feel frustrated that you have pay the locksmith to make a house call, but you can express your gratitude that you have a roof over your head. When you break your antique vase, you can be sad for the loss and thankful that you were able enjoy it for awhile. When your sweetheart dies, you can feel grateful that you were blessed with so much love.

Much of the twisted and toxic anger that we see displayed through violence, aggression, and war is due to this ever-present struggle—unconscious though it may be—to come to terms with the inevitability of loss and death. Marne, upset over her mother's untimely illness and death, found herself snapping at her sister-in-law until she realized that she was mad at the medical system and God. When she looked deeper, she found that her anger at God was preventing her from accepting the kindness of the many people who wanted to comfort her.

To find the spiritual lessons that anger can bring, we must be willing to see the bigger picture; we must shift our focus away from our inconvenience and upset toward the joy that is always present in our lives. We must step back from our anger so that we can be grateful.

Life and loss, beauty and death, love and anger are closely intertwined. When you react to everyday annoyances as if the world has just come to an end, it's a signal for you to explore life's bigger questions, to search for the spiritual nugget.

 The more anger a situation causes you, the more you need to look for the spiritual lesson it holds.

Walk the Higher Road

Because society needs people who conform to its norms, it imposes its rules and values on us as we grow up. The only thing we possess to counteract society's pressure is our feelings, and one of those protective feelings is anger. That angry voice inside you is like David standing up to Goliath—it calls you to right action.

You know you're on the road to healing when you start feeling angry. The anger may not be specific or related to anything you can identify; it may be a generalized anger that you can't pin down. Used in a positive way, that anger will empower you to move forward. "Aren't you mad that your husband died?" people asked me. I'd shrug my shoulders and say, "I don't know." Initially I was too numb to feel mad. It was only as I was getting better, coming out of the shock, that I started to feel. And I felt a wide range of anger, from mildly annoyed to downright infuriated. I realized that I would have to manage my anger or it could destroy me.

The higher road to anger management involves asking yourself, "What is going on here? What does it have to do with me? What do I have to learn? What positive impact can I make?" It's waiting, pausing, figuring out what is going on *before* opening your mouth, before taking any action. It's being grateful for what you're discovering.

Anger is a crucial shove toward determining priorities, values, needs, your bottom line. It's a beacon shedding light on the kind of person you want to be and the virtues you want to embrace. Taking time to consider how you want to live your life, what your needs and priorities are is walking the higher road. When you find yourself reacting like an explosive device, try stepping back and asking yourself these questions: "Is this how I want to behave? Is this the life I want to be living? Is this who I am?" If you find yourself chronically angry, it's a signal that you've been avoiding these questions.

How you feel is up to you. No one else has anything to say about it. And in a sense, it isn't even up to you. How you feel is simply how you feel. That's it! And when you *get* that, when you fully appreciate and honor that, you will instantly be a stronger and more fulfilled human being. Because even more important than what you feel is *how* you feel about what you feel. When you feel OK about your feelings, regardless of what they are, your self-esteem is unassailable and you're no longer mad all the time.

When you admit that destructive expressions of anger are causing problems in your life, then you're walking the higher road. When you find constructive outlets for your pent-up energy, when you demonstrate a willingness to do something positive and creative with your anger, you're becoming emotionally mature.

 Examining your anger and using it to understand who you are is right action. It puts you in the presence of the Divine.

Find the Fear

A burst of irritation, like spontaneous laughter, let's you know that you're alive. Being alive means you have lessons to learn, mistakes to make, challenges to face, painful growth to experience, and fears to overcome. Life is a glorious gift. Everything is divine, including me and you. We can learn from everything—even anger and fear.

After taking an anger management class, James acknowledged, "Most of my anger has to do with unmet needs and fears. I'd come home from work and if things weren't the way I wanted, I'd get mad. I alienated my wife and scared my kids. I know now that anger covers up my fear, but since a man is not supposed to be afraid, I'd get mad instead."

Anger seldom comes by itself; fear almost always accompanies it. Fear and anger are roadblocks to happiness. If you sense that you are standing on the sidelines while your life is passing you by, that's an indication that fear has taken hold. You have permission to hold onto fear as long as you want, but it will exhaust you and keep you from living. Fear paralyzes you. It wraps you in a blanket of passive resignation, unable to participate in life. Maggie is afraid of flying. She resents her friends when they take vacations and don't choose spots within driving distance. But so far she hasn't done anything about it except grow bitter.

Whatever you fear is the very thing that you must tackle. I don't mean that you must go bungee jumping because you're afraid of heights, but if you're afraid of flying, it could be beneficial to take a course. Afraid of applying for a job, anxious about calling your mother-in-law and asking her to baby-sit, afraid of talking to the dentist about the bill? Afraid of asking your boss for a raise? Whatever you are dreading, that's the thing you must face.

You may not be able to drop fear completely, but you can overcome it by getting comfortable with the sensations of fear in your body. When you're fearful you start to tremble and shake, to quiver and quake. Let the fear take possession. Enjoy it! If you're afraid of fear, you really will be paralyzed. You will not live totally. You may be attracted to woman or a man but you hold back, and soon you're missing life. Fear and anger are debilitating.

All self-doubts are based in fear. We think, "It's too late for me," or "I'd like to, but...," or "What difference will it make?" or "It's too hard," or "I'm too old, too fat, too ugly, not smart enough." It takes guts and courage to uncover the fear beneath resignation, but don't you think it's worth it?

 At the bottom of anger are two big fears—the fear of living and the fear of dying.

Take Grudges to the Dump

One way to rid yourself of the bondage of resentment is to write a "mad list" and then take your grudges to the dump. The purpose of a mad list is not to enflame grudges or to keep them burning, but to face them squarely, to see what constructive action you can take, and then let go of them once and for all.

In a journal or on a long roll of butcher paper (my women's groups like to use butcher paper and colored markers), write down all your grudges, resentments, hurts, and disappointments. Label your list: "Things That Have Made Me Mad, Hurt Me, Caused Me Disappointment." Trace the old nagging anger back to its root cause. Where does it come from? Whose voice do you hear? What happened? Divide your life into decades, starting with the first ten years, followed by the next ten years, and so on, until you arrive at today. Write everything down. Don't be picky; get it all out. Write as much as you can, then put it aside for a day or two. Come back to your list, read it over and add to it. Remember this is not the time for editing; it's OK to list all the picky little annoyances as well the major disappointments, hurts, and resentments. You're not hurting anyone by putting it out on paper. You're cleaning out, ridding yourself of garbage. Listing residual resentments gives you perspective on your personal history and the part you played.

If you sense that you have resentments but can't identify them, think about those times when you were mistreated and misunderstood, the times when you were overlooked and unappreciated. Chances are good that there's a resentment that's tied up with it. Think about your school years—there's plenty of misery tied up there. What about that love affair that ended unhappily? What has been your biggest disappointment in each decade? Write down your heartaches and regrets. Erica's list went like this:

> First decade: My parents liked my brother best. It's affected my adult relationship with him.
>
> Second decade: My parents got divorced; my brother had more freedom than I did. My mother remarried right away and I hated my stepfather.

Third decade: I married my husband and dropped out of college.

Fourth decade: I resent my husband because I really want to finish school.

After you've written your list, read it over and think about what part you contributed to the situations. Erica said, "My brother tries to be friends, but because I still resent him I don't give him a chance. I need to make amends to him. My stepfather tried to help me, but I felt disloyal to my father so I wouldn't cooperate. I want to apologize to him and my mother. I haven't expressed to my husband how much I want to go back to school, and I need to do that too."

Cleaning the storehouse of resentments frees you from the past. Instead of relating to her brother as if he is still Mom's favorite, Erica can relate to him as he is today and forge an adult friendship. Instead of feeling like a helpless victim of her stepfather, she can see how she contributed to the misunderstandings. Instead of expecting her husband to read her mind, Erica now takes responsibility for working out the financial matters so that she can complete her schooling.

Focusing on grudges is time-limited—devote one a week or at the most two. Write your list and clean up your part. Once you've done that, crinkle up the list, tear it to shreds, and take it to the dump.

 Anger is a useful emotion when it leads to personal awakening and compassionate action.

Confess Your Anger

Your first reaction will probably be to skip this one, but I advise that you don't. Remember that there's an entire religion based on the premise that confession is good for the soul. The fourth step of twelve-step recovery programs involves confiding your resentments to a trusted confidante. Even if you can't tell the person you are angry with that you are—maybe they're dead or you have a restraining order against them—you still need to tell someone. It's a two-part confession: You acknowledge how you were hurt and angered by what happened *and* you acknowledge the part you played. The purpose of doing this is so that you don't waste any more precious energy bottling it up. When you acknowledge your anger and the part you've played, you're no longer a moody victim.

When we share our concerns with others, it speeds up the resolution, it unites us in our humanity. We find out that we're not alone. We've all made mistakes. We can learn from each other, correct our faulty thinking, and move on. In the process we help each other.

Ask a friend if she'd be willing to listen to your "mad list." I suggest making an appointment so that you can devote as much time as you need to the experience. A secluded place out of doors—perhaps in a park, by a river, on a mountain, or at the beach—is a favorable site for a confession. Speaking it outside, where the trees and sky can hear you and absorb your resentments, is an empowering experience.

 The very moment you acknowledge your anger to another person, you are spiritually set free.

Beat a Drum, Play a Piano, Dance

Everyone enjoys a drumbeat. A drum is the most natural musical instrument. And when you're mad, nothing helps right away as much as connecting with the primal part of your being. Drumming helps you get out of your head and back into your body. Any kind of drum will do—just get a good steady rhythm going. If you don't have a drum, a round oatmeal box and the palm of your hand makes a wonderful noise. Beat gently. Not in an erratic way, but in a disciplined, measured manner. Spend at least ten minutes, and soon the beat will start going on its own. When you feel the drumbeat, your body starts to respond, you sway, you start falling into the beat, you move with the beat. Notice that when the beat of your heart and the beat of your drum are in step, you feel exhilarated. Your racing thoughts are slowing down. You can *feel* your body.

Although you can't learn to play when you're mad, playing can help you avoid getting mad in the first place. Many people who sit in front of computers all day are numb from the neck down. They know that they need to get back into their bodies. One way to do that is through drumming, playing the piano, or dancing.

It's hard for people with low self-esteem and blocked emotions to express rhythm. If you've been taught that you're dirty, you can't move your body to the beat. Dancing or learning to play a musical instrument teaches discipline while tapping into sensuality.

As children many of us had horrendous experiences with music that have tainted our view of ourselves. A choir director told one of her junior high students, "Just move your lips because you can't sing." Another told an eight-year-old aspiring drummer, "Playing drums is unladylike." Separated from our sense of rhythm, ashamed of our bodies, uncomfortable with our sensuality, it's amazing that we're doing as well as we are. William Congreve said, "Music hath charms to soothe a savage breast, to soften rocks, or bend a knotted oak." By incorporating music into your life you can change your hostile energy. Music gives you a positive way to feel what you're feeling without hurting yourself or others; it can smooth your ruffled edges. By expressing yourself through music, you're demonstrating a willingness to move forward, to let go of negative and hurtful behavior, and to find healthy ways to face the things that upset you.

Music is a natural stress reducer, a good joy maker; it's been shown to lower blood pressure and alleviate depression.

Make a tape or CD of the music that instantly elevates your mood, then next time you're annoyed or frustrated, play it and give yourself a lift. Sing in the shower. Join a choir or go to a concert, and you'll no longer feel so lonely.

Music is a communal thing. Perhaps the lack of belonging and lack of community that we're all feeling contributes to the rise of angry acts. Music brings people together, makes them joyous, lifts them up. Do you suppose that if we could make more music together, be more comfortable with our bodies and rhythm, that there would be less violence?

 Sing a song, learn to play an instrument, dance until you can't stand up. Then notice where anger has gone.

Cry

The tears that come with anger are cleansing. Crying is an energy phenomenon. Your emotions have been frozen, and suddenly they're thawing. Be happy about it. Crying releases so much pent-up energy that by the time you're finished you feel relieved, calmer, more at ease. It's as if the burden you've been carrying has been washed away by a river of tears.

I almost always cry when I'm mad. I used to feel ashamed about it, but I don't mind as much since I discovered that crying is actually good for the looks. That well-hidden fact is proven again and again in my women's groups, where crying is an honorable part of the agenda. When group members experience the benefits of weekly crying jags, they stop wearing mascara to the sessions. We first noticed the improvement in looks after Grace had a crying episode that lasted twenty minutes. Her husband had been laid off from his job at Boeing, and with three children to support money was tight. Christmas was around the corner and her youngest son needed oral surgery on his front teeth, which had been knocked out that afternoon in a skate board disaster. The dentist told her that she could pay in cash or charge it. Her credit card was maxed out, she was stressed out; life was looking pretty bleak. "It will work out, it always does," she cried, "but right now I don't know how." The financial burden threw her over the edge. "I hate dentists and teeth," she yelled. As she paced the floor, Grace recalled how her brothers held her down while her abusive stepdad pulled out two of her front teeth with pliers. Her horror story caught us all off guard. We listened in shock as she cried, "He pulled my head back by my hair, forced my mouth open and yanked out my teeth. I've never told anyone; for some reason I'm been ashamed about it." Grace cried and swore like a crusty old sea captain. She blew her noise, wiped the smeared mascara from her cheeks, sat down, and apologized, "I'm sorry," she said meekly. "I look awful when I cry." She sniffed and dried her eyes with a tissue.

"Your eyes are red, but you don't look awful," Joan said. "Your face looks softer."

Amy agreed, "You look so sweet."

"Your eyes are wide open," Linda piped in. "And you look younger."

"Crying is cheaper than a facelift," Grace laughed. "Since it's all I can afford, I'll have to stick with it."

Sobbing melts away the scowl lines. After a good cry your jaw and brow lines relax; the tightness in your face melts away, and you look softer, rejuvenated, and younger.

Tears are beautiful; they come from your core. When you cry, you start feeling that you're a mess because your identity is shaken. And as you cry, you become vulnerable, more open. Then laughter is possible. If you can really cry, one day you will really laugh. Tears and laughter are interlinked. Crying will help you relieve your tensions; laughter will help you dance and sing. If the first process has started, the second is not far away.

 Crying is good for your looks.

Shout Outside, Scream in the Shower

The pain of life can sometimes be so sharp that there's nothing left to do but scream. Elizabeth Kübler-Ross is well known for her work with death and dying. In her workshops she advocates screaming. I've witnessed a hundred group participants, who'd lost a loved one or were dying themselves, one by one in front of a room full of strangers hit a mattress with a rubber hose and scream. In her lectures Elizabeth talked about the benefits of cathartic screaming versus masking the screams with tranquilizers. If you can scream instead of deadening yourself, you might avoid years of torture. Primal Scream Therapy is based on screaming away the pain of birth and childhood.

Remember the famous scene in the movie *Network* in which the man throws open the window and shouts from the top of his lungs, "I'm mad as hell, and I'm not going to take it anymore"? Well, perhaps you have felt that way too. Something has disturbed *your* peace and now you want to disturb *the* peace. Step outside and shout loudly to the heavens. It's OK to raise your voice even if the neighbors may wonder what is going on, and at least you won't be shouting at your loved ones. If you roar from deep within your belly, you might be surprised at how empowered you'll feel.

Taking responsibility for anger by raising your voice in the shower is far better than raising your voice at strangers, friends, and loved ones. Open your jaws widely and let it out. You don't have to go into the shower to scream, but I find that water running over my aching body is soothing. Let it all out. Feel the sensation of the water running over your head and down your body as you release the pain you've held in far too long. You're not hurting anyone, and you're healing yourself. You're cleansing your body inside and out.

 A cathartic scream is therapeutic as long as it isn't directed at anyone.

Howl at the Moon

Have you ever cried out in anger, moaned in pain, wailed, sunk to the bottom of despair? Have you ever heard wolves or coyotes howling at the full moon? Have you ever wanted to join in the chorus? If you have, then you know the cleansing power of wailing. It's a melancholy hymn and, like singing the blues, it makes you feel better. It's a meditation. A call to pay attention, be conscious, an invitation to wake up. Howling at the moon might cause your neighbors to think of you as a bit eccentric, but so what? Howling brings peace—people stop and listen, haunting silence fills the air. Howling meditation releases the clutter in your mind. And that's worth any embarrassment you might endure.

After graduating from college, Scott went back home to live with his parents. He broke up with his girlfriend and agonized over what to do next. "I didn't know what I wanted to do, so I was working in a temporary job at a nonprofit organization. I was living with my less-than-understanding father, and since my attitude kept getting worse, it was making my already tenuous living situation very shaky.

> I'd been trying to keep a stiff upper lip, but one day, all the pressures came to bear upon my "pre-identity" psyche and I couldn't take it any more. I walked into the backyard, got down on my hands and knees, and for a good ten minutes I bawled my eyes out. I couldn't stop, and I bawled some more. In an ironic and touching moment, my dog came over and licked my face as if to say, "I'm your only friend right now, but I'm here for you."
>
> While lying on the broken concrete I had the thought and prayer (at that time my thoughts and prayers were one) that my elevator couldn't go any lower. I told God he could do whatever he wanted. I was broken and humbled.

The outgrowth was a new beginning. "Miraculously, my identity began to form," Scott remembers. "An identity not dependent on my father's approval or wishes for what my life should look like, but my own identity." Eventually Scott figured out a career direction and moved out on his own, married, bought a house, and found a great job. "But," he says, "it was that breakthrough moment that allowed me to become me. It was a shedding of something akin to youth's eggshell."

Any birth is painful, and we all go through birthing pains throughout life: those moments of agony when, as Scott puts it, "my elevator can't go any lower." Dark nights of the soul, existential fury, the blues and melancholy, hopeless dejection, pity parties, despondency, and angst are like birthing pains that free us from a shell that not longer fits so that we can grow into our new self.

 Wailing will help you relieve your tensions.

Run Around the Block

I've heard that in Tibet, they have a saying: if you're angry then just have a long run around the house and when you come back, see where your anger has gone. I've tried it myself and it works. Studies show that physiological arousal of anger is reduced by physical motor activity. Anger is best released with some good physical exercise.

Running eliminates unnecessary torturous mental gymnastics. If you run fast, your breathing changes; if your breathing changes, your thought pattern changes. Thoughts trigger anger, so anger is then reduced.

As soon as you recognize that you're feeling frustrated, cranky, ornery, stubborn, hateful, or negative, get moving. You can figure out later what you're thinking and feeling. Before crankiness and frustration has a chance to explode from every cell, get outside and start moving.

Warning: If you are resisting trying one of these techniques, ask yourself, "What am I getting out of staying angry? Is there some kind of payback in it for me?" Anger and catharsis can become additive. Some folks get obsessed with catharting; I call them "rage-o-holics." They make all kinds of mad gestures, and it's draining to be around them. They use their anger for gaining power, as a club over others. Catharting is not a goal; it's a means to a goal. Like a ferryboat, it takes you to the opposite shore. If you are always catharting and never dealing with the issue, you're in a vicious circle, on the verge of being known as a drama junkie and complainer.

 One benefit of exercise is that it decreases the thoughts that fuel anger.

Sit on the Ground

This is really important! You've been screaming, running, throwing a fit; your heart is beating, you're feeling the relief of a good workout. Now before you do another thing, find a comfortable place on the ground and sit down. Feel the earth beneath your body, holding and supporting you. Sink down to the ground. Touch the earth with the palms of your hands and feel how sturdy everything feels. Some people say that this is what being grounded is all about. As you're sitting there you're likely to feel safe and secure, knowing that the good earth is supporting you. What a relief when just a few minutes ago you were in a tizzy.

To get free of compulsive patterns, you have to create a kind of laboratory for yourself. The way to do that is to observe your own mind. By watching your thoughts, desires, and memories pass through your mind, you can identify the triggers for your anger.

Our minds are jammed with negative beliefs, thoughts, judgments, and grievances that can set the tone for the day. Notice how many times you point the finger at someone else by saying, "How awful!" or, "How horrible!" Or you scold yourself with "shoulds." When repeated again and again, these short words cement our thoughts in anger. To let go of anger, you have to let go of these self-defeating phrases. Jaime placed a rubber band around her wrist, and for one week, each time she used a "should" she lightly pulled the rubber band. By doing this, she became aware of how much she was keeping herself under pressure and irritated.

Our words and thoughts create our reality. Instead of weighing yourself down with "It's not fair," try saying, "It's a challenge." You'll feel less defeated and consequently less angry.

While you're sitting on the ground, you might consider whether or not you're carrying around the destructive belief that you're not good enough. There are corners in our psyche that are so touchy that any real or imagined criticism can send us over the edge. This is especially true if we doubt our own self-worth, if we think that we're not good enough. When we feel unlovable even the slightest rejection can hook into shame. When that happens we do our best to cover up by attacking, ridiculing, and pointing the finger. Later, of course, we feel worse about ourselves, and the shame-anger cycle continues. If you feel ashamed when someone is even the slightest bit angry at you, there's probably a shamed-based hurt inside that needs attention. If you sometimes think that something is wrong with you, you definitely need shame reduction.

Being outdoors lifts your spirits. While sitting under a tree, write poetry, listen to soft music, read Shel Silverstein to the squirrels. Walk into a garden, and suddenly you're in touch with another realm. Look at the flowers, smell the fragrances, hear the joy of birds singing, watch the peaceful swaying of trees. Sit quietly for a moment and take it all in. In a garden you can get sensitive, open, vulnerable, and available to natural order. As you pull weeds you become in tune with the rhythm of life and discover peace and oneness with the world. Whether it's a pea patch or an entire acre, there's a sense of connection and accomplishment after planting.

 While sitting on the ground, create a laboratory for yourself. Witness the traffic in your mind, and discover what thoughts stimulate your anger.

Lie on Your Back

Have you ever noticed that when you're angry, your entire body seems to tense up? One way we've learned to repress our anger is by tensing up. Tensing up leads to stiff necks, headaches, and tight chests. Staying mad is the opposite of relaxing. When you relax, you let go of the idea that you need to do something. You simply drop the whole notion of getting even or fixing what is wrong.

When lying on your back, your body starts to relax, and if you breathe deeply, your body will begin to quiver. Please allow the shaking and twitching. It's your body's way of releasing blocked energy. It shows that you're getting ready to open to healing, and it's a good indication that natural healing energy is flowing. As you lie there, notice that your back is being supported, be aware of whatever sensations you feel. Pay particular attention to the area in and around your eyes; let the built-up pressure melt away. Continue to notice your breathing.

Watch angry thoughts come and go without trying to influence them in any way. Don't try to change anything; when you notice an angry thought, such as "I can't stand her" or "I'll get him," say to yourself, "Aha!" and let it go.

Imagine that the various parts of your body are inflated balloons. Your foot is an inflated balloon, your fingers are inflated balloons. Now imagine that all these balloons have valves and that air is being let out of these balloons very, very slowly. As you let go, listen to the sounds around you. The wind through the trees, the birds chirping, a dog barking, the sound of your breathing. Notice what you missed while anger stole your attention.

Lying on your back and releasing pent-up tensions is not the same as becoming a couch potato. A couch potato vegges out in front of the television in order to ignore what's going on inside. He may zone out for awhile, but his body stays tense. Turn off the television and count the people who love and support you. You are loved and supported by many people.

 When you learn how to relax, you won't be able to stay mad.

Kick and Make a Noise

Hold on and don't freak out with this suggestion. Yes, you read it right: Start kicking. While lying there on your back, notice that your body and legs want to move. Bend your knees and keep your feet flat on the floor, and start kicking. At the same time make two fists and pound on the floor. This is what we call a temper tantrum; many body-focused therapists recommend these techniques to clients who want to free themselves from all kinds of repression, including sexual. Rumor has it that orgasms can be better in a body that is not afraid of its own energy. Yippee!

Now, speaking of great orgasms, the same experts report that the people who will allow their bodies to express whatever noises come up are also better lovers. So with that encouragement, while you're on the floor, kicking and pounding, let whatever noise you want to make come out loudly. It might be a scream or a growl or deep sobbing. You can get the process rolling by pounding your fists on the floor and saying loudly, "No, no, no."

It doesn't matter what noise or what words you scream, but that you allow the noise, the words, or the scream to come. Don't edit anything. There are moments when everyone wants to scream. Children seem to understand this—it part of their language. So although you may think that screaming is irrational, remind yourself that it's natural and good for your sex life.

If you've ever turned the water back on after the pipes have been shut off for a long time, you know what happens: the pipes make a creaky, banging, gurgling, clanging noise before the water starts flowing. Initially, the water comes out in spurts and is brown and rusty, but then the water gets clearer and the creaky noise lessons. Eventually the noise stops altogether, and pure water flows. The noise and the rusty water make way for the pure, clear water to flow once again. We are like pipes that have been turned off too long. For our energy to flow easily, before we can feel our sexy selves once again, we have to kick and make loud noises

 A wise man once said, "Laugh and the whole world laughs with you; stay mad and you sleep alone."

Look to the Sky, Pray for Direction

If you've ever been mad at a friend or a relative and then talked about it with everyone except the appropriate party, you know how powerful the process can be. You can build a case against anyone—even your dearest friend. Since Cain turned against Abel, sisters spread rumors against sisters, parents cut children out of wills, relatives disown relatives, in-laws wage war and gossip, neighbors sue neighbors. If you tell your side of the story without giving the other person a chance to tell theirs, you'll find plenty of people agreeing with you. "Yup!" they'll say. "He's bad, she's wrong." You'll have no trouble justifying your position. Righteous indignation is like a snowball: when you're packing it on, it grows larger.

You can talk till you're blue in the face, but unless you're willing to go directly to the person with whom you're upset, you're only being sneaky. It's OK to talk things over with a third party as long as your heart is open to both sides of the story. While it's good to reflect on the words you want to say and how you want to deliver them, it's not nice to tattle, gossip, or spread rumors. When you're trying to fortify your position by pointing out how nasty your friends or family members are, you're being rather nasty yourself.

Changing a spiteful habit is a spiritual process of humbling yourself and asking for guidance. You can't transform a bad habit by willpower alone; you'll need grace and good guidance to do it. By accepting that you can't resolve hurt and anger on your own, you invite a greater force to intervene. When people pray, they often look to the sky for guidance and direction. The sky is very symbolic of Spirit, which is always present. Looking at the sky, you somehow know that all is not lost. In fact, when you can look up instead of down, you're beginning to find your way.

Look to the heavens and hold your head up high, seek reconciliation, pray for forgiveness. Let your thoughts come and go. Meditate on the sky. You're part of the universe, and so are your friends and enemies. We're all part of the Great Spirit. Watch the birds that come by and imagine yourself flying. This is much better than spending hours waging war and justifying.

Sadly, some folks relish hearsay and scandals. They like to pretend to have all the answers. They're proud, they have big egos.

Joseph Campbell said, "Sad is the man who doesn't know about the unseen forces in the universe." There are many unseen hands ready to assist us whenever we ask. By praying instead of gossiping, we surrender to a power that is larger than we are. We acknowledge that we aren't in charge of everything.

You don't have to say any fancy words when you pray. A simple prayer straight from your heart will do. "Dear Heavenly One, I'm angry at my mother. Please reveal to me what I need to do to heal this upset between us." When you pray you surrender to the power of the universe and you open the way for peace and love to arrive.

 When you're angry, pray about it, ask for guidance, wait for the answer, then follow the advice.

Say "Yes" and "No" Frequently

The baseline for much of our shrouded anger is locked-up desires, hidden wishes, unfulfilled longings. Tears of frustration, mild depression, free-floating anxiety, and downright unhappiness cover up our secret aspirations. We think the good life is for movie stars, artists, or the more intelligent. We doubt ourselves, we're sure we don't have what it takes. Paralyzed with worry that others will judge us as selfish or brazen, we postpone fulfilling even the simplest desires. Soon we're afraid to try. So we lock our dreams away and feel cheated. We become lethargic, live through others, feel irritable and defeated. Our expression turns sad, our eyes turn green with envy, our gaze becomes blank. We're angry but don't know it, or if we do know it, we don't want to admit it, and we never, never want to show it.

What do you want to do with your shrouded anger? Are you content with the status quo? Do you want to retreat from life, or do you want to seize it? Materializing dreams means saying "No!" to what you don't want, so that you can say "Yes!" to what you do want.

No is a very important word. Why else would a two-year-old spend an entire year learning to say it? We all have to learn to say "No" to what doesn't fit, so that we can say "Yes" to what does. Elizabeth said, "No, thank you," to her mother-in-law, who wanted to take her out for a birthday lunch, so that she could say "Yes" to the way she really wanted to spend the day—-staying in bed and reading.

Some folks say "Yes" when they mean "No," and vice versa. What they're left with is free-floating anxiety. Frustration, anxiety, and anger are triplets. Anger is specific and directed at the other person: "I'm mad at you." Anxiety is nonspecific and directed inward: "I'm anxious and irritable, but I don't know why." Frustration is an interruption that gets in the way of getting what you want. Consciously saying "Yes" and "No" eliminates all three.

Anger, anxiety, and frustration have a lot to do with how you approach life—as a choice or an obligation. If you experience life as an obligation rather than a choice, anxieties and resentments are bound to build up. That's how folks get filled with indignation.

You've probably heard stories of people who've decided to cash in their saving and sell their belongings and live on a sailboat. Perhaps you know someone who has simplified their lifestyle by moving to the country. You've may have been inspired by those courageous souls who, despite physical handicaps, learned to ski. We all have choices—we can say "Yes" and we can say "No."

We can follow our own hearts. Even though we're afraid and have no idea of what the outcome will be. Others may laugh and mock us, and we might fail, but won't it feel great if we succeed? And having a vision of how great that would feel, every step becomes a thrill.

 Try this anger-reducing exercise: For one week, say "Yes" and "No"' clearly and frequently.

Say Good-bye to Baggage

Over the years, my various housemates could tell when I was angry, anxious, or frustrated by how intensely I cleaned the house. When things were going downhill, I'd wax the floor or polish the silver. Whenever I'm really mad, lost, bored, or disgusted, reorganizing the cupboards cleans out cobwebs from my brain. I clear out the junk in the garage, I sort the clothes in my closet, I throw away papers. By getting rid of the old I make space for something new.

Oprah has said that once a year she cleans her drawers and cupboards; at the same time she goes through her phone book and clears out the phone numbers of acquaintances or relatives whose negativity brings her down. She wants people in her life who lift her up. A healthy relationship is one that inspires you. Do an inventory of the people in your life. Do they lift you up or tear you down? Are they positive or negative? Do they take responsibility for their own anger, behavior, attitude, and choices, or do they blame others?

If you have hateful negative people around you, you will be influenced by them. If you're hanging around with folks who wallow in muck, that's where you'll be wallowing. All those grumpy, hostile, cranky, sarcastic, cantankerous folks who love to give you a hard time are frustrated. They're encumbered with irrational beliefs that they haven't cleaned up. Complaining together keeps you both feeling grimy. Like kitchen cupboards that need cleaning, our attitudes and thoughts need a thorough going over.

While you're cleaning the closet, clear out your emotional baggage at the same time. Box up those irrational beliefs that keep you spinning. While you don't want to hang out with negative friends or be around folks who put you down, avoiding annoying acquaintances altogether is not the final solution. It's our own grandiosity that really keeps us stuck. Staying cool in the face of life's aggravation means that you have to admit that the majority of your anger is brought on by your own inflated idea that others should always treat you well. We humans seem to have the conviction that we're so special that others should see it and treat us like kings and queens. When they don't, we get mad. When you think that someone should give you special treatment and they don't, that's when things turn hostile.

You can live happily without fame and fortune, without limousines and maid service. When you accept that you are no more special than anyone else, you can clean the house and feel good about it. Then you can encounter life's injustice and remain friendly.

 When you know your own worth, there's no need to be mad if others don't treat you well.

Bring on Forgiveness

Rosie told me her story of forgiveness:

> My father and I didn't get along. If there were two sides of
> an issue, he'd be on one, and I'd take the other. Talk about
> anger! That man had an accomplished temper. I honestly
> don't remember very much violence from him, but his
> threats struck terror into the hearts of my brothers and me.
> His shouting and fuming caused real harm. My parents
> would shout and argue, and as a child I'd cover my ears
> and hide. When they weren't arguing, Dad treated my
> mother like the maid we didn't have and she'd comply. In
> my late teens, I'd beg her to divorce him, but she just said
> that wasn't her way.
>
> Then Dad got sick, a long, mysterious, complicated brain
> disorder. My mother had to provide twenty-four-hour
> nursing because he refused to go to a convalescent hospi-
> tal. After eight years, he had a stroke and had to go into a
> nursing home. I visited my dad every two weeks, even
> though he was unable to talk or respond. Finally I got my
> nerve up to talk with him, not knowing if he could hear
> me. I told him it was time to let go, that the doctors said
> he wouldn't be getting any better, and that he should feel
> good that he'd lived a good life, had many friends, and
> that his family loved him. I couldn't tell a dying man that
> there wasn't much love left.
>
> Dad died, and a few days later, my brothers came from out
> of town to pay their last respects. The church in the memo-
> rial park was filled up. It was true that he had lots of
> friends, from every segment of his life—work, hobbies,
> convalescent hospital. He had been a good friend, even
> though he hadn't shown that warmth to his family. When
> the minister didn't arrive, the coordinator said we'd better
> go ahead with the service. My mother turned to me and
> my brothers and said, "You do it. But please don't say any-
> thing mean."

A do-it-yourself funeral was the last thing we'd had in mind. My brothers were overcome with nervousness and emotion and were unable to say much. I stepped up to the front of the church, looked at the people, and said, "My father would have hated this." Everyone laughed, because it was true that Dad was a stickler for things being right. From then on the service went fine. We had the prayers and the music; I described his life story, leaving out any anger and hate. I didn't lie, but I just said whatever neutral or positive things I could, emphasizing what a good friend he had been to so many. It was a wonderful service, and a great way to close my relationship with him.

So what if we didn't get along? Should I let that define my life? At the close of his life, there arose an opportunity for me to be free from him and free from anger toward him. The anger had never been good in any way, and I was glad to be rid of it. When the minister finally showed up, after the service had ended, I hugged him.

Happiness begins with the understanding that holding onto anger doesn't do you any good. We're all capable of doing terrible things; we're all imperfectly human. By accepting our own defects of character, we can forgive others. Forgiveness is not ignoring the hurtful words or actions that wounded you; rather it's opening your heart wide enough to see from a larger perspective. It's understanding that anger hurts the perpetuator as much as the victim. When you forgive and are forgiven, you open the way for happiness to come in.

 Forgiveness means to accept yourself and the other person as is, no grudge, no complaint, no grumbling.

Select an Antidote to Anger

Whenever I'm bewildered, irritable, impatient, down in the dumps, or flat out mad, I put on my favorite version of "Amazing Grace" and I listen to it over and over again until I can't remember what was annoying me in the first place. Listening to "Amazing Grace" lifts my spirits, and I can let go of petty annoyances and find compassion. In the big scheme of things, most of what irritates us is either imagined or insignificant. When I'm trying to control what I can't control, when I'm taking myself too seriously, listening to Art Garfunkel and his son James singing "Good Luck Charm" opens my heart so wide that I feel as if I can make room for my enemies.

We can't control what others think of us; in fact, what others think of us is none of our business. Our business is to get over getting mad, to balance the pressures of life with pleasure, to partake in whatever lifts us up, to lend a helping hand. Pansies with smiling faces, cats purring, hanging out with a friend, floating down a river, helping a stranded motorist change a flat tire, volunteering at the soup kitchen, smiling at a stranger are all antidotes to anger. When you find yourself scowling and complaining about what you don't have, it's warning sign that you're so wrapped up in what's wrong that you can't see what's right. It's an indication that what you've been pursuing is not fulfilling you, that you've been blowing your circumstances way out of proportion.

Antidotes to anger neutralize aggravation. Continual angry feelings and thoughts keep the adrenaline pumping; this can have long-term consequences on blood pressure and the health of your heart. Here are a few anger remedies:

1. When someone puts you down, don't take it seriously. It's just one person's opinion, and they've probably been wrong many times.

2. Read jokes and give them away. My friend Cliff Durfee sells Sprinkles by the thousands. Sprinkles are paper cutouts such as hearts, stars, and smiley faces. I specifically like the G-rated jokes printed on tiny strips of colorful paper. (You can buy them at www.livelovelaugh.com).

3. Counting to 10,000 does help—as long as you count slowly and breathe. So does singing or saying a mantra. You will still have angry thoughts and feelings, but this technique keeps you from putting your foot in your mouth and making matters worse.

4. Eat a piece of chocolate. Lola and her husband were arrested for domestic violence, and as part of their sentencing they had to attend anger management classes. Lola learned that one of the triggers for her husband's violence was her smart mouth. After that, whenever she felt like saying something nasty, she popped a Hershey's Kiss™ into her mouth to remind herself that if she couldn't say anything constructive it was better to keep quiet.

5. Carry a peace medallion. Choose a small stone, a shiny agate, or a medallion, and carry it with you to remind yourself that it's natural to have angry thoughts and feelings, but you don't have to open your mouth and prove it.

6. Run for your favorite smell. A calming scent such as lavender or rose oil, a sprig of fresh lavender, cedar chips, or the aroma of freshly baked bread can do wonders for your disposition. When you're on anger overload, aromatherapy might settle you down.

 What others think of you is none of your business. Your business is to get over getting mad.

Join the Secret Society of Satisfied Souls

My friend Chloe turned sixty while I was writing this book. She said, "I just can't seem to think of anything that gets me riled up enough to be angry anymore. The anger and pain I've felt about things in the past is either gone, or feels like a little ripple with no juice in it."

My sister-in-law Cathy told me, "Since I'm not mad, it's hard to conjure up the memory. I think over the years I've done just about everything: pout, scream in the car, talk about it indignantly and self-righteously to everyone except the appropriate party, cry my heart out, visualize the person's face on a golf ball (amazing how that improves ball contact), write in a journal, see a therapist, meditate, go jogging, call the person."

A former client told me, "When I was young the only emotion I knew was anger. If I wanted to talk with someone, I'd get in a tussle to do it. If I was sad, hurt, or worried, I didn't let anyone know. I wouldn't let anyone put one over on me. I was mean. Fortunately, I've outgrown it. My wife, kids, and grandkids tell me I've softened."

Good wine mellows with age. Perhaps we mellow with seasoning and the awareness that nothing creative or constructive comes from staying mad. As we mature we learn to face life's challenges with a light heart. It's through experience that we discover how laughter gets things moving in a positive direction quicker than griping. In a crisis, it's Grace that shines light on the solution. Cry when you're hurt, use anger as empowerment to fix what you can, let go of resentment, laugh, and move on. When you can do that you've joined the Secret Society of Satisfied Souls.

The Secret Society of Satisfied Souls have earned their diplomas. They've sobbed their broken hearts out in crying class, they've stomped and yelled through anger management, they've laughed at their own foibles. They've graduated and learned to love. They're experts in living. The Secret Society of Satisfied Souls now work for the Institute of Love.

Satisfied Souls from the Institute of Love are always available. If you need to cry, they'll hold your hand. When you're mad, they'll set you straight, and although they'd never force you, they'll make every attempt to protect you from yourself. Satisfied Souls like to sing and dance. You can spot them by the twinkle in their eyes and the spring in their steps. They know just the right moment to tell you a joke. They point out life's absurdity and chuckle along with you. The Secret Society of Satisfied Souls bow to *all* of existence; they celebrate life to the fullest, and you, dear friend, are always welcome; you have an open invitation to attend their parties.

 In the end you are who you are—discombobulated and cranky or happy and satisfied.

PART 2 In the Presence of Your Sweetheart

A trustworthy person is angry at the right people, for the right reasons, expresses it in the appropriate manner, and for the appropriate length of time.

—THOMAS AQUINAS

Our love relationships are filled with experiences of profound harmony and union *and* experiences of great clashing and discord. We're often most angry at the people we most love. Our beloved disappoints us; we're enraged, infuriated, and ready to fight. We hurt each other without intending to and sometimes with intention. We put on our armor and go to war without ever leaving the house.

Anger unites and separates us in the most intriguing ways. Most of us have, at some time, lost it, blown it, freaked out, behaved unreasonably. When anger is expressed in a straightforward manner, it is the simplest of emotions. But because human beings are so complex, the expression and repression of anger becomes complex and quirky.

Adam and Suzanne have very different styles of expressing anger. In front of others, Adam appears mellow and never raises his voice, but behind closed doors he yells. He's easily frustrated, throws tools, slams doors, and punches the wall. He's seething inside; he's lonely but doesn't know what to do about it. Suzanne is verbal, good at debating; when she gets angry, she talks circles around him, then blames him for withdrawing and for being so cold. They have a lot in common, and when they get along life is wonderful, but when one of them is angry, life turns horrid.

You'd like to get along with your partner and behave lovingly all the time. You feel better when you do, yet no matter how good your intentions, how diligently you try, you fall short. You lash out, you say snotty things, you're sarcastic and cruel. Sometimes you're cold. Your partner tries to be loving to you, but when he gets frustrated he takes it out on you. You get mad, you fight, you say mean things, you blow up, and then things really escalate. You say the one nasty thing that you didn't mean to say and you're off to the races. You feel crummy for hours—sometimes days. You don't like the tension between you, and you want to make up.

Perhaps it's been this way for years; you've been having the same old argument since the honeymoon. "The first fight we had," said Christy, "was about the fact that he can't say 'No' to his mother, and we've been having it ever since." You promised yourself the last time that you wouldn't get caught again, but you do.

You will fight. You will get angry. You won't get along. You'll see things differently. You'll wonder why you married each other. You'll decide she's the most difficult woman you know; she'll be convinced that you don't care about her anymore. When your husband talks to you like no one has ever talked to you, when you've called him a name that you're mother would shudder at hearing, that's when you're in the thick of things. Angie summed up her situation: "We never get angry and we never make love."

It's not that you shouldn't fight; it's that you must. You can't smooth out *all* the wrinkles, but you can smooth out some. You won't agree on everything, you won't find perfect unity all the time, but you can agree to disagree. You'll argue over the inconsequential— like who forgot to put the cap back on the toothpaste and who put the roll of toilet paper on backward; you'll fight about lifestyle preferences—whether to save money or spend it, whether to buy furniture or a new car, whether to have sex or go to sleep. You'll disagree about the children, the budget, the relatives. But that doesn't have to mean the end of happiness; it's how you manage your anger and the sore spots that will make or break your relationship.

See Relationships as a Great School

Human relationships are a great school. What do they teach? They teach you that your partner has to be considered. That your beloved, with whom you share so much, is different from you. They teach you many things, and ultimately they teach you that *you alone* are responsible for your behavior and for making your life meaningful and fulfilled. When you stop expecting others to make you happy, you still get angry but you don't stay mad.

Expectations are often a source of friction. One person says, "You promised," and the other person makes excuses. And then both become self-righteous, each insisting that he or she was right.

Often, when people first get into a relationship, they've been yearning for one. They've been eager for companionship, eager for some tender loving care. Most people come into relationships with high hopes and dreams. And they're excited because they've found someone who is going to fulfill those dreams. Then the partners have their first disagreement. It's not a fight yet; it's only a disagreement. They're still trying to be nice to each other, trying to understand and be courteous. Many of their feelings don't get expressed, and afterward, frequently, there's some resentment. And then one day they have their first real fight. They're not just discussing; they now admit to some real disappointment and differences. Maybe they even get angry.

They start expressing feelings they haven't ever expressed before, feelings they never even knew they had. They try to work them through—and they hardly know what that means at this point—then the bond between them gets deeper, and they become more committed. When deeper issues come up, once again, they work things through. That's how a relationship gets built. That's how trust develops. The disappointment and the anger and the hurt all get transformed in some way, and it's nothing less than miraculous.

 We learn the most about ourselves from the hardest teachers, who often are the people with whom we've chosen to share our lives.

Learn from Arguing with Your Partner

In the twenty-five years that I've been a family therapist, I've collected, with the cooperation of my clients, accounts of some outstanding quarrels. I've asked husbands and wives to write down their fights and bring these accounts to me. I've included some of them in this part of the book. Reading them is fascinating and instructive.

There's a conspiracy of silence about anger and fighting, quarreling and making up. Nobody really talks about it. The subject is a closely guarded secret. Couples and families are very tight-lipped about what is going on behind closed doors. So, just in case you thought you were the only one who gets angry and has big battles, I've got news for you: You're not. Very respectable people get angry and fight. Here's one of my favorite quarrels, which I have heard in various forms. My clients and I have named it "You Never."

Mark says, "You never want to make love." Carla replies, "And you never help around the house." Mark and Carla have fought the "You Never" quarrel in one form or another for sixteen years, and although they haven't solved every one, they've figured out that most of their complaints about one another are linked. If he's feeling "you never" about her, she's probably feeling a form of "you never" about him. "I've learned that if I want sex, it's a good idea to help around the house," Mark says. "And I've learned that if I want Mark to help around the house; he's more willing if he thinks we're going to have sex," Carla says.

Love and anger, fighting and making up are the absolute nitty-gritty of human existence. What can you learn about getting mad and making up? What can we learn from our quarrels and from reading those of others? To avoid the pitfalls! To recognize strategies of domination and techniques of manipulations—regardless of whether these are your own or someone else's, and regardless of whether they are deliberate or only semi-conscious. To see the patterns that lead to conflict.

To recognize and avoid those patterns requires considerable skill, but learning about yourself and how you've contributed to the mess you're in is easier in the long run. If you're willing to learn about yourself, you'll still disagree with your sweetie, but you'll do it in peace and goodwill.

If you've ever snapped at your sweetheart because she was snapping at you, you know what a negative chain reaction that little snap can set off. If you've ever raised your voice in reaction to the tone in his voice, you know firsthand that two shrill tones don't make an agreeable melody, or a congenial marriage. There is a Chinese proverb that says, "If you are patient in one moment of anger, you will escape a hundred days of sorrow." All couples have arguments. The trick is to be patient during the argument. Patience in the middle of an argument is the passkey to understanding what the trouble is about. When you're patient, you can treat each other gently while figuring it out. And often you don't need to figure it out at all, because being patient with each other was the only remedy needed. All arguments can end kindly with the words, "Yes, dear," or "I see what you mean."

 A satisfying relationship is not accidental; it happens with plenty of listening, laughter, quarreling, and making up.

Recognize the Value of Anger

The ways of love and anger are very unpredictable. Sometimes people yearn for love without finding it, and sometimes they simply fall into love without even looking for it. But regardless of whether they've yearned for it, planned for it, or just fallen into it, lovers know that love feels wonderful. Everything is so delightful, and you feel so exhilarated that you can't imagine things will ever be different. And yet things are different, or become different, very quickly!

Lovers do get angry with each other and start fighting—sometimes very soon after they first get together. Getting mad at each other and quarreling is just about inevitable. It goes with the turf.

I once asked a well-married friend of mine whether he had fought with his wives. "Yes," he replied, "I did, but not nearly as much as I should have." He reminded me of an important finding: that the way a couple deals with anger and conflict is an important factor in determining the success of a relationship.

You can deal with conflict by shoving it under the rug, by pretending it doesn't exist. You can deal with anger by overpowering the other person—whether you do it with a club or by sweet-talking them into oblivion.

I know people who don't even *hear* remarks they don't want to hear. They're convinced that anything that may possibly lead to friction must be tuned out. They insist on nothing but sweet talk. They're right to a point: All the sweet-talking lovey-dovey stuff is great—but unfortunately, it doesn't last forever. Anger and conflicts need to be dealt with. If you don't deal with them, they gather momentum until one day nothing can stop them, and they then thunder down upon you like an avalanche.

 Anger is a signal that something between you needs to be dealt with. Paying attention to what's troubling your partner is good for your relationship.

Pin the Blame on the Donkey

There are all kinds of fights and plenty of things to get mad about. Money, sex, raising kids, religion, politics, where to live, in-laws, vacationing, drinking, eating, health—it's just infinite what people argue about. All these quarrels express themselves in different ways—hot anger, cold withdrawal, rivers of tears, and violence. At the bottom there is one thing that characterizes all quarrels. And that's The Blame Game.

The blame game is also known as fault-finding, nit-picking, making the other wrong, criticizing, complaining, bitching, whining, and seeing the mote in the other's eye. We play the blame game for many reasons. No one likes to admit being wrong. We say, "No I didn't," or "It's not my fault," or "That's not true," or "Well, look what you did." Blame is like a hot potato—we toss it back and forth. She says, "You spend too much." He says, "You're too tight." She blames him or the circumstances; he tosses it back.

You can make a case against anyone, and that includes your beloved partner. In love relationships the tendency is to blame the other person for our feelings: "You made me angry." Then we replace that with: "I feel angry when you do such and such," which is still pointing the finger at the other person. Anger arises to help us get to the root of the matter, but we have a tendency to blame the other when we're angry rather than looking within ourselves or at the problem. If something is not happening as we'd like, it is easier to blame the other than to take responsibility for getting what we need.

Remember, you're always responsible. If he is 75 percent to blame, that leaves 25 percent for you, and that's the part that you must deal with. If you don't like what's going on between the two of you, change yourself. Drop those qualities or actions that create trouble in your relationship. Make love a self-transformation, and your life will be enriched.

We can't expect our partner to do it all or be it all for us. We have to look deeply within ourselves to find what needs to be changed. Instead of making the other person wrong, communicate about what is causing your pain. That's more productive.

Is all this blaming really worth it? In the blame game, both players are losers. You'll be much happier if you pin the blame on the donkey. The blame game stops when one person says, "I see what you mean," or "I never looked at it that way," or "You might be right." The blame game stops when one person says, "Honey, lets pin the blame on the donkey instead of each other."

 I know a husband and wife who filed for bankruptcy, lost their house, their cars, and their business. Instead of blaming each other, they threw a pity party. The invitations read, "It's our party and we'll cry if we want to."

Create a Safety Zone

The ties that join a loving couple are far stronger that the forces that divide them. Loving couples create a safety zone where anger can be expressed without either getting hurt. Their relationship is not threatened by disagreements. They're aware of each other's strengths, they value what each brings to the union; consequently they won't let anger fly out of control. They take care of each other even when they're fighting. "Let's not go there," Sean reminds his wife, and together they make a turn from the dead-end direction they're heading.

Couples who manage anger well function under these principals:

1. Physical violence is not allowed. Loving couples have an irrevocable rule against physical violence. They may get into shouting matches, but they would never hit each other, throw things, or destroy each other's property. There's a mutual respect for each other's point of view, and even when they're in the heat of an argument, there are places they won't visit. They don't insult each other's mothers or call each other names.

2. Our goal is what's best for us. Loving couples know that the goal of arguing is to clarify what is happening. If one person is angry, the other partner wants to find out what is going on rather than winning. They know that proving yourself right tears you further apart; trying to understand what life is like from your sweetie's point of view solidifies your union. Happy couples work to find a solution that is good for both.

3. Assume positive intention. Happy couples use anger as a signal that they need to sort through the muddle and find clarity. When one of you is angry, you both feel bad. A positive intention is to resolve it so that you can both feel better. When your partner is mad about something, don't assume that you know what it's about. Making assumptions before you've heard each other out is deadly to a happy resolution. When your partner is angry, instead of assuming the worst, come to each other in a spirit of cooperation. This gives you a far better chance of a positive outcome: "What's best for us."

4. Our differences are our gain. When you finally admit to yourself and to each other that you have differences, you'll feel anxious, uneasy about your relationship and wondering if it's going to work out. When you're angry that your spouse wants to sleep with the window open while you prefer it closed, know that the negotiation that goes on between you is what having a relationship is all about. There's nothing wrong with feeling frustrated that he doesn't do it your way, but avoid the trap of thinking that the reason your life is so difficult is because of him. Instead of saying, "We can't get along," say out loud, "We're having a difficult moment," and then add, "Let's figure out how to create something superior out of this." Instead of trying to erase differences, a loving couple finds ways to incorporate elements of both.

 Loving couples disagree and get angry, but they follow principles when fighting so that they don't destroy each other in the process. They strive to resolve their arguments so that they both feel better.

Intend to Stay Connected

It's crucial for couples to disagree without disconnecting. A commitment to each other means an alliance, a standing together to face whatever comes—including loving, quarreling, and making up. It's not outside forces that threaten to divide you; the biggest danger to your union comes from within.

Trigger-happy, dart-throwing, firecracker types, Jack and Leigh came to counseling ready to fight. If Jack loses money playing poker, Leigh claims her right to spend an equal amount of money on clothes. When she (against his wishes) invites her family to visit for a few days, he (against her wishes) flies to Las Vegas. Regardless of what happens, they insist on their individual rights first and foremost. They get mad when they don't get their own ways.

It's productive to get angry, disagree, debate, and fight it out, as long as your intention is to understand one another better. You will have differences of opinion. You'll have ample frustrations. You'll get mad and quarrel, but those tussles don't have to tear your relationship apart. Remember, it's love that all of us are seeking.

Instead of fighting for your own way, fight for the kernel of insight, look for the clue that brings you closer, make your intention the search for mutual understanding. Seek to find out all that you can about what makes yourself and your sweetheart tick. You can fight the same old fight over and over again—as most of us do—and remain optimistic. By agreeing in advance that you will hang in there even though you risk being exposed, you establish positive intention.

When Todd and Alice designed their new home, it was an artistic undertaking of combining his preference for an austere rambler with her desire for a cozy two-story cottage. He wanted sleek gray slate for the entry; she wanted whitewashed stone. He likes black leather straight-lined furniture; she wants white brocade slipcovers. "We had plenty of heated disagreements, but we've ended up with a home that incorporates both," said Alice. "We combined our preferences for black and white and came up with a gray theme. We combined smooth surfaces with texture; we incorporated elements of each taste and found a balance. This brought a harmony that wouldn't have been there without each other's contributions." You expand your horizons by combining the best of your distinct preferences.

Regardless of how angry you are, chances are you'll stay connected by remembering:

1. Don't say everything you're thinking or feeling, because if you do you're likely to cause another fight.

2. Say something positive about the situation: "I'm glad that we're in the process of figuring this out."

3. Always apologize when you're out of line: "Honey, I'm sorry, I goofed."

4. Stay hopeful and restate often your intention to stay connected.

 Instead of fighting for your own way, fight for the kernel of truth that brings you closer.

Use the Practical Approach

When your upset involves your partner, give him a clear picture of what is going on. Tell him—as soon as you figure it out—what you're thinking and feeling. When your sweetheart doesn't know what you're thinking or feeling, you're both in the dark. Not sharing an opinion, an idea, or feeling that's intense and important to you automatically creates a distance between you.

It takes courage to good-naturedly tell our mate what we're concerned or worried about. That's especially true if she has a position that is different from ours. We imagine that he will be bothered by what we have to say, and since we're uncomfortable with arguments, we avoid bringing up our differences. Nothing gets resolved and the distance between lovers grows. Sooner or later the pushed-away upset seeps out—either through sarcasm, resentment, or constant bickering—and by then the original disturbance has been compounded with more frustration and misunderstanding.

Expressing yourself well is difficult at first, especially if you haven't had much training in the art, but it's worth learning. By your expression you can reshape the core of your relationship. When you keep your upset a secret, it eats away at your self-worth and your relationship can't improve, but when you use anger as a positive force for change, you can resolve what's bothering you.

Here are five easy steps for expressing yourself to your mate:

1. Ask if she is willing to help you solve a problem: "I'm wondering if you could help me with a problem?"

2. Make a statement about what's upsetting you: "I'm feeling overwhelmed with my responsibilities and I need to have quiet time each evening to unwind. When you interrupt my reading it's difficult for me to relax."

3. Ask for the changes you'd like your partner to consider: "Could we agree to an hour of private time each evening?" and "Would you make sure the kids don't interrupt me?"

4. Share what you're going to do differently: "Before I take my hour of private time, I will check with you to see if you need me to handle something first."

5. Thank your sweetheart for listening and considering your request: "Thank you so much. I appreciate your support and understanding."

If you carefully consider the statement you want to make before making it, the effort is usually productive. Even if it doesn't get the results you wanted, you will feel good that you spoke on your own behalf.

 If you want to talk about an emotionally charged subject, it works best to ask, "Honey, is this a good time to talk?"

Give Yourself and Your Loved One Freedom

A strange phenomenon sometimes happens in love relationships. Many couples, once they've found each other, try to hold on and squeeze so hard that they have no room to breathe. Well, this simply doesn't work! We say, "When will you be home?" And then when our sweetie is even a few minutes late, what do we do? We rant and rave, scream and yell, throw a fit. And if our honey wants to spend a day with a friend, we stomp our feet and pout—we threaten and accuse—and love slowly fades and withers into resentment.

Finding the right balance of togetherness and separateness is part of the task for a couple. When Elaine feels stressed, angry, or worried, she wants more togetherness, while Greg needs distance. "I need more time outs then Elaine does," says Greg. "When I'm upset, I need to go to the gym and work out before I feel like being together."

Freedom is very important in managing anger. I'm not suggesting that you take a back seat and become passive while your mate has an affair, but I am suggesting that you let your lover have the freedom to process the anger and hurt that he feels.

The real reason that we object to our loved one having freedom to process their feelings on their own is that we're afraid—afraid that sooner or later they'll leave us. But the quickest way to ensure that they indeed will leave us is to insist that they always and forever relate only with us.

You also have to give yourself freedom—the freedom to be true to yourself. That can be very scary. Maybe you'll get into trouble. Maybe somebody will get mad at you. Maybe something embarrassing will happen. When you're not true to yourself, you're not really happy. You think the other person is to blame, when not being true to yourself is making you unhappy. And when you're not really happy, you start feeling resentful, and you're quick to anger. If you're not true to yourself, instead of feeling love you start feeling resentful—and the wall of resentment between couples is hard to take down.

 Loving partners allow each other freedom for self-exploration.

Watch Out for Time Bombs

There is the normal expression of anger—-you bark at your wife because she volunteered the both of you to chair the church committee; you give your husband a tongue lashing when he's late for the lunch he invited you to—and there's the chronic, toxic anger that's a carryover from the past. Healthy anger is short-lived. Some research indicates that the anger response lasts about a minute. Which means that tirades of anger are an indication of a slush bucket of childhood wounds and "stinkin'-thinkin'."

Living with a chronically angry person is a like living with a ticking bomb. You know that they're about to explode, but you don't know when. You don't want to trigger their rage, so you walk on eggshells and live in constant dread.

Brad has a problem with anger, but he doesn't know it. He's anxious, tense, and can't sit still. At night he plops himself in front of his big-screen television with a six-pack and barks orders to his wife and kids. If the kids are too noisy, he sends them to bed early. He verbally abuses his wife. He's impatient, gets annoyed easily, and shouts out threats.

Allison has a problem with anger too. She smiles and takes tranquilizers. If she doesn't get her way she's cold and critical. She tries to please everyone. When anyone gives her feedback about how her behavior is affecting them, she's defensive and interprets it as an attack. She verbally attacks back. If her children talk back, she falls apart, cries, and locks herself in the bathroom.

Both persons are time bombs, bubbling with rage. Rage may stem from repeated physical, sexual, and emotional abuse in childhood; abandonment by one's parents through neglect or absence; an unsafe emotional environment that didn't allow for the natural expression of feelings. Rage can also arise from social isolation and trauma. Rage is stored at the cellular level. It distorts our temperament and flares up out of nowhere. Here are four warning signs of untreated rage:

1. The person can switch from an easygoing mood to an angry mood in seconds, without any warning.

2. The person expresses anger by hitting, throwing, shoving, grabbing, pinching, or punching.

3. The person uses name-calling, threats, and criticism.

4. The person is impatient, gets annoyed easily, is quick to use put-downs and poke fun.

Untreated rage destroys relationships and makes it impossible to have a happy, peaceful family life. You can't enjoy each other when one of you is eaten up by untreated rage. Rage is different from healthy anger in that it requires professional intervention, sometimes years of therapy, to work through. If you're in a relationship with someone like this or sense that you're suffering from pent-up rage, I encourage you to seek counseling right away. If you're living with a person full of rage you know it. Your gut tells you that something is wrong.

Wives and husbands are equally capable of treating each other miserably. Your spouse can only abuse you if you allow it. It's really true that it takes two to tangle. If you're in an abusive relationship, get help now.

Throw Out Old Patterns

Each of us comes into a relationship with emotional conditioning, patterns for dealing with anger that are left over from childhood. Many of us were not taught how to put words to our feelings; we weren't taught healthy ways to resolve anger or deal with conflict. You've learned a certain style for expressing anger, and chances are that the person you married has a pattern that's different from yours. How did your parents show anger? How did they resolve differences? When your parents were angry, did they tell you directly what was going on or did you have to guess? If they were mad with each other, did you suffer? Whose pattern do you tend to follow?

Lynne was raised with parents who never fought. "The first time Rick and I had a fight I just assumed we were headed for the divorce court," she said. "Later in life I understood that my mother harbored so much anger and resentment because my father wouldn't fight. He sulked instead and used his arthritis as an excuse."

Tim's parents never showed anger directly. As an adult he gets nervous and avoids anyone who does. His wife feels frustrated, because if she raises her voice or gets the slightest frustrated, he hides in the garage. Kate grew up with a raging mother, so she thinks it's normal for her husband to yell at and criticize her; she doesn't express her own anger and makes excuses for her husband's threatening behavior.

While childhood sets the stage for what we learned about expressing anger, our adult relationships are determined by our own choices. By sharing your childhood experiences of anger, you and your spouse can figure out what will work best. Do you want to resolve your disagreements as your parents did, or try something different? Which of your parents expressed anger and which one kept it in? Which parent are you most like? What is your anger style? Do you vent anger quickly or let it simmer?

Most couples say that handling anger constructively is the hardest part of their relationship. Resolving the little frustrations, hanging in to complete a heated discussion until both are satisfied, takes years of practice. Ashley said, "When we were first married, Nick would disappear when I got mad, which only made me madder. Then I'd yell and throw his papers on the floor. Now after thirty years of marriage, Nick still disappears when I get mad, but I leave his papers alone. I wait to talk with him about it until I can put my anger in perspective. Then I try to be logical because he can't handle my emotions.

"My mother told me, 'Never go to bed mad.' It was the philosophy we lived under. But Nick will wait weeks to talk about what's bothering him. So we've compromised. I've learned that if I wait until we've both cooled down, he's better able to express what's troubling him. I don't like waiting a week, but I've waited twenty-four hours. I've gone to bed mad and found out nothing bad happened." Postponing is often better.

 A wise person once said, "If your spouse makes you angry wait a day. If you're right, then you can have a good laugh; if you're wrong, then you can apologize."

Master Conflict, Not Your Partner

Remember, in marital conflict, your spouse is your ally, not your enemy. When a couple full of anger, fighting, and blaming comes to me for counseling, one of the first questions I ask them is, "Do you want to be enemies? Or do you want to be lovers?" Then I remind them that enemies handle conflicts differently than lovers do. Lovers are loyal to one another, they struggle to stay together; enemies clash and pull apart. Lovers are willing to give up their own claims to the truth and to walk in each other's shoes.

When conflict and anger persist in your relationship, it's an indication that you're both longing for appreciation and attention. Each of you wants to be cared for and cherished by the other. When you're not getting the understanding that you need, you feel hurt; then you cover the hurt with anger and start duking it out.

Disappointment and hurt are predictable, but the pain doesn't have to become entrenched. Instead of overpowering your partner to avoid the hurt, reach underneath and find out what's troubling you. You can change the pattern of constant bickering and even violence by recognizing that you want the same thing from each other—respect, kindness, and a little understanding.

Think about when you first came together. Didn't you go out of the way to make each other happy? Your partner is not the problem; the problem is that you've forgotten how much you have to give to each other, how much you really need each other. Hurt couples get very competitive, jealous, and suspicious, and they stop doing the very things that bring them love and comfort.

Here are four homework assignments to help you shift your focus back to what brought you together in the first place.

1. Cooperate with your partner. Instead of fighting and getting angry, be agreeable. Instead starting an argument, stop one.

2. Make a conscious effort to give your beloved words of appreciation and encouragement every day. Something as simple as saying, "You can do it!" can turn a day around, can turn someone feeling down and discouraged into someone who is happy and enthusiastic. Praise them for learning to do something new even when they haven't quite got the hang of it yet.

3. Choose a day that will be "Treat Your Lover Lovingly Day." Don't tell your beloved which day it is—just choose it, and then your treat your lover lovingly for the entire day. Let it be a surprise. And make a point to treating your lover differently on that day than you do on the other days.

4. Do something for yourself every day! Never skip a day—and be sure to ask your sweetheart what they intend to do for themselves.

 Master your fear, jealousy, pain, and rage, not your partner.

Pause

There are times when pausing, waiting, and taking a time out is necessary. Once you're mad and the adrenaline is flowing, it takes at least twenty minutes for the body to slow down enough for you to think clearly. Distance gives you an opportunity to cool off and find out where you stand.

When you're having a battle that keeps going round in circles, ask, "Is this really what we're mad about? Is this really the issue between us?" Sometimes we get mad at little things when there's something beneath the surface that we haven't addressed. A time out helps you clarify what's going on within yourself and gives your spouse the same opportunity. You can always re-address the issues later. Lauren says, "Time outs are helping me learn to balance being an individual with being a couple. I used to think that everything I felt had something to do with Clark. Now I'm seeing that what I'm feeling might only have to do with me."

There's a difference between reacting and responding. Some couples are so reactive that I call them "firecracker couples," because if one of them gets angry they both get angry; they react to each other like a string of firecrackers popping off in many directions—chaotic, noisy, and jumbled. Firecracker couples are quick to jump on every word, expression, tone, and innuendo; this leaves them unable to see their own parts in the string of events. Taking a cooling-off time lets you see how your reaction triggers each other; it lets you get clear about your part. You can't change the other person's reaction, but by taking a break, you can change your own, then you can respond instead of popping off.

Agree in advance to time outs. It's OK to take time away, but reassure each other that you'll be back to talk it over.

Work It Through on Your Own First

Have you've ever been irate, stuffed it, and then suffered with a splitting headache? Have you ever been furious and taken it out on a stranger? Have you ever had a bad day, then snapped at your husband? Have you tried to overlook what was bothering you? For every minute you're angry you lose sixty seconds of happiness. Staying mad is a sure way to miss out on pleasures.

While you don't want to waste precious moments grumbling, you can't ignore what's annoying you and expect to be happy. You have to consider the issue directly, solve it quickly, and then move on. You don't have to work everything out between the two of you; you can work some of it through on your own. You may not even have to encounter your partner until you have changed inwardly yourself.

Chronic anger is a signal that you need to look deeper. Ask yourself:

1. What about this situation disturbs me? Is there anything else?

2. What's going on in me?

3. Before I say or do anything, what can I learn?

4. Who is responsible for what?

5. What things do I want to change?

Anger can be about many things. You don't like what's going on and want to straighten it out. You've doing too much for your family and need time alone, you want more time together, or something your partner said reminded you of something your mother used to say.

Unfortunately, some people never explore what the problem might be. Instead they blow up, let off steam, and feel vindicated by the temporary relief. They forget to take care of what triggered the anger in the first place. When you recognize that you're angry, look inside yourself to see what is troubling you. Then find a solution so you don't have to keep going over the same old territory year after year.

 Recognize when you're angry and try this strategy: Say, "I'm think I'm getting angry." Then pause and say, "I need time to think over what's going on in me before I can talk to you."

Master Timing

If you've ever had a complaint dropped on you when you're in the middle of a novel, if you've ever had an upset brought to your attention while you're putting the final touches on dinner, if you've ever fallen asleep to your sweetie's complaining, then you know that timing is important. The wrong timing can get you sidetracked from a meaningful conversation.

There's nothing wrong with spontaneously venting our anger as long as we are not abusive and hateful, but sometimes blowing up does nothing to resolve long-standing patterns. Waiting for the right moment is not only good for relationships and individual growth, but is the basis of anger management, managing our impulses to sling insults back and forth.

"Honey, we need to talk," may get your honey's attention, but if you insist—when your partner is not in the mood—you'll both feel frustrated. Lots of arguments start in passing and gain momentum because you haven't been respectful of what's going on. You're angry, you spout off, and whether you meant to criticize or not, your beloved feels attacked and on the defensive. When you're angry, you want instant relief, but if you don't want your partner to feel battered in the process, you'll wait and choose the best time for the discussion.

 Sometimes all that is needed is a simple, short, clearly thought-out request such as, "Honey, will you please_____?"

Seek a Joint Perspective

If we want to grow spiritually, we have to take full responsibility for our anger, what triggers it, and how we express it. We must examine the root cause—what's behind it and where it comes from. If you approach your relationship as a creative journey in which you're growing and learning, exploring the lessons of anger together will benefit your mutual development. When you love someone, you want to learn as much as you can about yourself, so that you can become a better person and a better spouse.

It's important to talk with your spouse about how the two of you will handle anger. Are you going to view anger as "his," or "hers," or "ours"? There's often a pattern in relationships that goes something like this: She gets mad, he stays cool, or vice versa. The couple considers that whoever is mad has the problem. A more satisfying way of looking at anger is from a joint perspective. If one of us is mad, then we both can benefit by talking about it, finding the cause, and solving the problem. Instead of saying, "That's your problem," and leaving it there, a couple interested in mutual growth says, "It's our problem." If one partner is mad about something they address the issue together.

Sydney comes from a family who gets angry easily. They enjoy arguing over dinner; they abuse each other with words. They consider it sport. Philip never heard an argument from his parents, whose eventual divorce came as a complete shock. Sydney and Philip want to handle anger with out hurting each other. They don't want to sweep disagreements under the rug, but they don't want to pound each other either. Instead of allowing anger to come between them, they want to use it for mutual growth.

When what we want doesn't match what our partner wants, when you think he's being stubborn, when your ideas for resolution make sense but don't pan out, that's when an important conversation is needed. Can you reach beyond the disappointments, let go of your anger, and laugh about the quirks?

 Consider either partner's anger as a problem to work on together.

Admit It

Most people don't like to admit when they're angry. If you ask them, "Are you mad?" they'll deny it. But their vibe and body language says that they are. Folks who say they never get angry have put in place a defense system of denial. Unwillingness to admit when you're angry is a surefire, foolproof way of reducing the connection between you and your partner.

When you're angry, admit it. First to yourself. "Yes, I'm mad and I don't agree." If you don't admit to yourself that you're upset, then you'll put off dealing with is the problem. You'll lose touch with yourself and the issues. Then anger leaks out in roundabout ways, in sarcasm and sneakiness. Admitting that you don't like what's going on is the first step toward change.

Next admit it to your partner. "Yes, I'm mad," or "Yes, I feel angry at you," or "Yes, I'm angry, but it's not with you." When Nathan asks Abbey, "Are you mad at me?" and she answers, "What makes you think so?" he feels that she's playing games, but when she answers, "Yes, I am," he feels closer to her. When she acknowledges that the angry vibes he's sensing are indeed there, he feels glad that at least they're operating on the same wavelength.

When you can tell others about some of the quarrels you've lived through (without blame but simply as entertainment or as scientific investigation), you'll both start feeling better about yourselves and about all your relationships. You'll find out that you can look at yourself objectively.

 Admitting anger is not bad. Because anger has caused so much pain, people go to great lengths to avoid expressing their own annoyances.

Avoid Revenge

Perhaps more than we would like to admit, we all use anger to cover up our pain. Zeus and Hera sure went at it. When Zeus' love affair with Alcmene produced a son, Hercules, Hera spent a lifetime getting even. She sent two snakes to kill baby Hercie in his crib, and when that didn't work she waited until he grew up, and at the moment of his greatest triumph she zapped him with a spell of madness. You can't blame Hera for being hurt and mad at Zeus for his philandering, but did she have to persecute the children?

The devastation that we experience when our beloved doesn't understand or seem to care leaves us feeling so utterly abandoned that we instinctively set out to survive by fighting back. "If I don't protect myself who will?" becomes our battle cry. The only defense we think we have is to get angry, get even, and strike back. And so we take care of ourselves by being angry. We torture one another. Some lovers wage war with physical brutality, slapping and pushing; others shrewdly launch verbal weaponry, calling names and belittling. Yet others scheme cleverly and threaten, while those more sinister use taunting and teasing. Many don the cloak of perceptual victim.

When we're hurt and seeking revenge, we're desperately isolated yet clamoring for connection. Secretly we hope that the one who hurt us will hurt as much as we hurt. If they do, surely they'll see the errors of their ways and come back pleading for forgiveness. When one of us, or both of us, is brokenhearted we yearn for the other to console us. We yearn for the very one that hurt us to come running back, promising never, never to hurt us again.

When we have hurt each other, that's when we most need comforting. Taking care of each other in the middle of the hurt and anger is a generous gesture, an act of reconciliation, of charity and compassion. Instead of exchanging petty crimes, abuses, ill treatment, and insults, consoling the person who has hurt you and letting them console you breathes new life into your relationship.

 When you're angry at your spouse, instead of plotting revenge, try planning consolation.

Lighten Up

Newlyweds Clint and Liza were bickering daily, discovering that going around and around trying to be right can ruin a perfectly lovely day. "We're both very stubborn," Liza admits, "and when we disagree even about the tiniest fact—like whether the upholstery is brown or tan, which side of the street to walk down, or who to vote for in the primary election—we can waste a whole day staying mad." Clint agrees, "We correct each other over minutiae."

Clint and Liza are discovering how many things there are to disagree about, and since they don't want to waste days arguing over the inconsequential, they've made a rule: "If we're getting mad, one of us says out loud, 'Pickle's feet!' and that changes our mood and the direction we're heading," Liza said. "Yesterday he yelled at me three times, 'Pickle's feet,' and I yelled back, 'Pickle's feet to you too!' It's working because we're laughing instead of snarling."

Every time you're caught up in nit-picking, say something nonsensical. Find a phrase that you both agree upon or a word that makes you laugh. That little ritual will make you more alert to the insidious habit of "making each other wrong" that's so injurious to love. Instead of assassinating each other's character, swallow hard and say something like, "Tickle, tickle" or "Puff, puff, puff."

Words have the power to provoke. A careless phrase can shatter your beloved's self-esteem and leave your relationship in shreds. "It's your fault," "You can't do that!" "You're wrong," "You can't do anything right," "Shut up!" "You don't know what you're talking about" are tiny bombs that have lasting impact.

Finding a common language for discussing hurt and anger changes the chemistry between you. "I want to understand," or "I see what you mean," or "I never looked at it that way," or "You might be right" are soothing phrases that turn the toxic energy from bitter to sweet.

 When you no longer insist on being right, it's an indication that you're growing up. Then you can disagree without nasty words, you can agree to disagree, you can feel angry without hurting each other, you can have a fight without being mean.

Move to Easy Street

One of the first homework assignments that I give couples who are full of anger and fighting is, Move to Easy Street for a Day. Walk easy, talk easy, think easy; let anger come and go. Sometimes we get angry because we push ourselves to do more, we compare ourselves to others, we strive for perfection. On Easy Street, we stop comparing ourselves and we deliberately slow way down.

On Easy Street people still get angry, but they let anger point the way to a deeper part of themselves. They take charge of the anger by identifying the fears underneath. Instead of letting the anger handle them, they recognize their own emotions but don't allow the emotions to rule. No person is without anger and no relationship is without conflict, but on Easy Street you don't blow it out of proportion and act as if the end has come.

A productive, easy fight is one in which you learn something new about each other, gain a new insight into yourself, or discover a more creative solution. It's telling each other in a kind way how you feel: "I felt unloved when you forgot our anniversary," or "I feel as if you don't appreciate what I do." It's admitting, "I goofed," and saying, "You right, that was thoughtless of me," without being overly hard on yourself. It's making amends: "How can I make it up to you?" It's kissing, hugging, and making up.

On Easy Street anger and conflicts are handled with care. Quarrels and differences of opinions don't upset the entire day, don't spoil the mood. Learning to use anger to clarify your relationship is a slow and gentle process. It's knowing what you're upset about, listening, negotiating, apologizing, and making up. On Easy Street you go easy on yourself and your sweetie.

I think that the Almighty wants our relationships to be easy. Certainly easier then they are when we're waging a free-for-all. Remember, anger gives you information about yourself. On Easy Street, anger isn't used as a club.

 Each time you stop yourself from lashing out, when you treat your partner as you would like to be treated, you transcend your human tendencies.

Turn Arguments into Intimate Dialogue

Anger gives us the opportunity to have an intimate dialogue. It isn't only good feelings that lead to closeness, but rather being able to talk about a wide range of human emotions and experiences.

Anger is a surface feeling. It never comes by itself; other feelings—hurt, fear, jealousy—accompany it. Beneath the surface of anger is hurt, followed by fear and backed up by love. For example, Lisa is angry at her husband, Mark, who locked himself in his home office all day after he'd promised to take her and the kids to the movies. She's angry at him for going back on his word; she's hurt and disappointed by his behavior; she loves him and appreciates how hard he works supporting his family, but she's afraid that his workaholism is becoming a pattern.

Some couples make the mistake of only hashing out the anger without talking about the feelings that accompany it. By leaving out the hurt, fear, and love, they rob themselves of an intimate dialogue. I like to think of intimacy as "In-to-me-see," which means letting your partner see you at your deepest and most honest core, revealing all that you're experiencing. If you only express the surface anger, you miss the opportunity to deepen the understanding and bond between you.

To have an intimate dialogue and process your anger, try using this five-step blueprint:

1. Acknowledge the anger: "I'm angry that you didn't take us to the movies as you had promised."

2. Acknowledge the hurt: "I'm disappointed because I really enjoy our time together, and I'm hurt; I'm feeling neglected."

3. Acknowledge the fear: "I'm afraid that your work is coming between us and interfering with family time. I worried that you're not taking care of yourself."

4. Acknowledge the love: "I appreciate how hard you work to support our family financially."

5. Acknowledge your part: "I'm sorry that I yelled."

How do you arrive at intimate dialogue? By wanting to. By recognizing that you are capable of it. Even if you've never done it before, you can learn to do it. Expressing anger, hurt, and fear without harming yourself or others is a healing process that leads to greater intimacy and compassion for each other.

When we're angry, we often put on a mask and act as if we don't care. Intimate dialogue is taking off the "I don't care mask" and letting your mate know that you do care. Because even when you're angry with them, you do care. If you didn't care, you wouldn't be angry in the first place.

What is intimate dialogue? Lovers can disagree, argue, and get mad, and the love can still be there. A lovers' quarrel doesn't have to be the end of the world.

Use Magical Phrases

When feelings are running high, when you're exhausted and the frustration level is at a roaring boil, instead of hurling insults, offer some gracious phrases to infuse your relationship with respect. Since you don't want to hurt each other, remember that grievances are resolved more easily when you're respectful. When you're respectful, you bring assurance that it's safe to be vulnerable and open your heart. When you're sure that he doesn't love you anymore, when you've asked her a thousand times not to call you names, before you threaten to get a divorce, before you wage a belligerent counterattack, before you sink to the lowest level, try these magical phrases. These expressions implicitly let your mate know that even though you're angry, the respect that you have for each other makes it safe to disagree.

> "Honey, I have a complaint/concern/disagreement/upset/ annoyance, and I would like to talk with you when you have time to listen."

> "I'm concerned about some things; can we set aside a time that's convenient for both of us so that we can talk things over?"

> "I want to give you my undivided attention. Can we schedule a time so that I can listen fully?"

> "I appreciate that you're willing to sit with me and listen to my concern. Thank you."

> "I'm not asking you to solve this problem. Right now I'd just like you to listen and give me your attention."

> "Is there anything else you would like me to know?"

> "What would you like me to do?"

> "I'll think that over and get back to you on...." (Be specific.)

> "Would you think about what you'd be willing to do to solve this situation? I'll think about some solutions too."

> "Let's get back together later in the week to continue our discussion."

"Thank you for bringing this to my attention."

"Thank you for giving me your attention."

"Together we can find a solution; we'll figure it out together."

It's not the end of the world if you get angry and argue; it goes with being together, with being intimate, with loving one another. It's what you do when you're mad that makes the difference. You can get very angry at each other and still appreciate the fact that you both want things to get better, to go smoother. The point is not to stop disagreeing, but to disagree and welcome the opportunity to figure out a brilliant solution.

If you stop talking to your partner because you're mad, you will probably be very lonely. If you negotiate your differences, you will probably have more company.

Experience the Contentment of Letting Go

Wives (and husbands) come to me and ask, "What can I do? My husband (wife) doesn't want to change—he (she) doesn't even want to hear about any of my concerns." This is a tough situation. I don't know what they can do, and I freely admit it.

But then I say that incredible changes are sometimes possible in one spouse if there is a significant change in the other. If a wife lets go of her ideas of how things ought to be, a husband will pick up on that and eventually respond. When she isn't being pulled hither and thither, when he neither whines nor pleads, when she frees herself from codependency, when he isn't being pressured, something unforeseen can happen. Sometimes, a result that you ardently desired but couldn't achieve emerges seemingly by itself, except it's even better. There is contentment in letting go. When we let go of our fixed ideas, the world changes. When we let go we feel better, more at ease.

Anger tends to pull us away from the person we want to be close to. To avoid this, we sometimes blind ourselves to what's going on. We relate to what we want to see, not to reality. This keeps us even more distant. It's in accepting our feelings, talking our differences over honestly, that we really get close.

This kind of fighting can sometimes enhance love. With self-assertion and good honest fighting, you get closer, you become more loving. You make love more often. And with some practice, fighting ceases to be something terrible. You get to a point where you can laugh about your fighting just as much as you can laugh about your lovemaking. Then it's just something you do that adds a little spice.

 Letting go of one's expectations of a partner can lead to remarkable changes in a relationship.

Set Each Other Straight

My friend Jay called me up the other day and said, "I'm concerned about something. Can we talk about it?" A couple weeks earlier I'd said the very same thing to him. It's simple. We're annoyed and we say so. Then we sort out our differences, fight for our needs, and set each other straight. He's late and I'm more or less on time, and while I usually don't mind his tardiness, sometimes I feel he's been taking advantage of my good nature. Then I get miffed and set him straight. For my part, I have a tendency to rush in to finish his sentences, assuming that I know what he's about to say. Usually he laughs, but once in a while he gets cranky and sets me straight. We can tell by the intensity and amplification if his tardiness and my talkativeness are the main issues or if they are covering up something deeper.

Have you ever consider that the stumbling block in your relationship might be you? We all need to be set straight once in a while; you're very fortunate if you have a reciprocal agreement to do that for each other. Setting each other straight is the unveiling of our blind spots, not in a "rub your face in it" way, but rather in a mutual, "Let's look at what happened here" investigation. If your partner is angry, it may be for a sound reason. Instead of being defensive, you'll get much further if you can accept feedback from each other. Acknowledging your weaknesses and admitting your mistakes is a sign of strength. Feedback is hard to take, but it's an essential element in creating the best relationship possible.

Anger can show you parts of yourself that you might otherwise miss. By looking at the dynamics between you, honoring both of your needs and tendencies, you have a blessed opportunity to uncover the messages that anger brings.

It's a wonderful thing to been seen and set straight. Often we think it's our partner who is messing up when it is really ourselves. When our partner gets angry and tells us, we're lucky. Some couples never set each other straight; they go their separate ways instead.

 It's a blessing to be in a relationship where you can set each other straight without devastating each other. It allows you to discover the truth in a spirit of mutual inquiry.

Apologize

All of us have, at some time, covered up, distorted the truth, ranted, pointed the finger, and tried to present ourselves in the best possible light. We've all heaped anger on the ones we most love. We're all human, we're all guilty of being cruel. We've all dumped the frustrations of the workaday world on other people. And we've all needed to apologize for something.

Anger smothers the flames of desire. Without an apology for hurt that's been caused, passion grows dim, and eventually resentments and heartbreak replace what once was excitement. If you wish to keep passion, desire, and interest alive, consider apologizing. A sincere apology can wash away the damage you've caused. It's a stepping stone back to your loved one's heart. When you apologize even though you think your partner treated you badly, you admit that you contributed to the mess. An apology soothes the bruises, melts away misunderstandings. By taking responsibility for the pain your anger has caused, you take a step toward reconciliation.

When you apologize, your honey feels cared for. In paying attention to the smallest detail, you acknowledge how important your sweetheart is to you. "I'm sorry I yelled, I know that scared you." Acknowledging your flaws, the nasty little things you do, the mean things you say is what being responsible is all about. You reap the benefits, too. When you apologize for the hurt you've caused, your own anger diminishes. You're happier, your step is lighter because your conscience is clear.

Albert Ellis, in his book *Anger: How to Live With and Without It*, says, "When you have an angry outburst, don't let yourself get away with it." If you have a problem with anger, ask your mate to help you deal with it. Make a plan to manage anger so that you don't hurt each other any more. When you make a sincere effort to rid yourself of hostility, you make your relationship sweeter.

Follow your apology by following through and following up. Follow through with your actions. Your actions are the reassurance that it's safe to be around you. Next time you're angry, don't slip back. Do whatever it takes to change your ways.

Follow up by making sure that your partner feels resolved. "Honey, is this issue resolved for you?" How are we doing with this?" Suggest, "Let's check back later to see how we're doing." Check back and ask, "Honey, are you OK?"

If you behaved badly in front of others— your children, the neighbors, the in-laws, your friends—the right and appropriate thing to do is to apologize to everyone who felt the fallout. They were affected by your outburst as well and therefore deserve your apology. You might say, "I yelled at your mother and that was hurtful and embarrassing to her. It was wrong of me. I have apologized to her and now I'm apologizing to you."

 When you behave badly, apologize to everyone who was affected by your actions.

Forgive When It's Time

Sometimes you can't forgive until you've gotten a little revenge. I don't believe in taking a pound of flesh, but I do advocate doing something for yourself so that you can put the matter to rest. Gracie Allen did just that when she found out that her husband George Burns had had a brief fling. She never confronted him directly, but she bought a very expensive chandelier and hung it in their dining room. She told him the trophy hanging over the dining room table was a reminder to him not to mess around again.

Jill's inability to forgive her husband for an affair that ended many years ago was creating a wide gulf. Jill's daily forgiveness rituals weren't working, and she was turning spiteful. "How can you get even?" I asked. A light bulb went off and Jill answered, "I don't want to go on the cruise with Charley. I want my girlfriend to go in his place. I want to spend his share of the money." Charley agreed to the plan and stayed home; Jill took her friend on the cruise. When she returned Jill felt vindicated. She and Charley kissed and truly made up.

It's very difficult to enjoy life if you're holding onto a grudge. Sometimes we have experienced so much hurt that we are unforgiving without being aware of it. Being unforgiving makes you're distrustful. The process of preserving an open wound—which is what not forgiving is—keeps you separate and very lonely. Keeping anger going after the issue as been resolved—muttering, complaining, grumbling—only reinforces your angry outlook.

You can build a case against anyone—even someone you left long ago. Unless you can forgive you will always be living in the past. And in your mind you will rehash the old hurts, disappointments, humiliations, and wrongs that were done to you. Soon you will be living in misery. The past cannot be changed, but it can indeed poison this most precious moment.

Paige and Lyle went through a bitter divorce seven years ago. Paige is remarried, and even though her new husband Matthew has never raised his voice or been dishonest with her, she doesn't trust him and keeps her guard up. She repeats horror stories about how awful Lyle was. Lyle has taken responsibility for his actions and completed two years of anger management classes. Lyle has moved on while Paige is holding on. By reliving the past over and over she thinks she's preventing it from occurring again, but she's only keeping it going.

True forgiveness allows you to accept your past and move on. It means laying to rest your animosities toward the people who have harmed you. You no longer try to change them, you no longer judge them, you simply, honestly, with no malice, accept their human shortcomings. You no longer blame them, you don't point your finger, you don't make them wrong. You forgive them, not so much to make life better for them, but so that you can move on. Your forgiveness takes the spotlight off the wrongs they've done and puts it on the action you need to take for yourself.

Forgiveness leads us to the redemption of our spirit. Even if the other person doesn't change their ways, forgiveness helps us grow, heal, laugh, understand ourselves better.

 To forgive someone who's hurt you, you have to see something other than the betrayal. You have to be able to see the growth in the other person.

Bask in the Thrill of Making Up

The thrill of making up is not only that you kiss and make love—the real thrill is when you see the absurdity of it all and can laugh about it. When you can disagree and not strike out, that's the lasting thrill, the joy of being a couple.

She looks at him, he looks at her, and suddenly everything is all right again. That's a poignant moment. And there is no way they could have had it without the argument. That's why a lot of people fight—because there is nothing like the thrill of making up. If you've never done anything bad, how can you ever experience the sweetness of being forgiven? So fight all you want and enjoy it. Conflicts are inevitable in marriage. The challenge is not to avoid arguing, but rather to know what you can do to end the argument and be closer. If your intention is to win or to hurt each other or to be right, you will never have the thrill that comes with making up. But if your intention is to appreciate the differences between the two of you, then you can reconcile without resentment.

Can we somehow put an end to quarreling and fighting with the people who are dear to us? I think pure love is the solution. Love without conditions and expectations. Not perfect love or divine love. Just appreciating one's partner without conditions or qualifications, seeing something wonderful in the other and approving of it—enjoying the other without trying to change them. Don't you love your puppy without conditions? Don't you love your baby exactly as he is? Can't you love a kitten without expectations? And if you can do that, why couldn't you love your husband or wife without conditions?

Without conditions doesn't mean without demands. Sometimes we do need to make demands. That's very normal, natural, and healthy. And we can withhold rewards too—sometimes that's necessary to get what we want. We can withhold the amount of time we spend with them or how much attention we give them. But we will withhold the degree of our participation, our energy, and our attention, not our love. We may get angry about something they did, but we will not close our hearts to them. We will find ways to honor them even when we are angry. We can clash with them on many issues, just as long as our love for them is not an issue.

Recognize that you are love at your core and that your anger is a residue of wounds that may go back far in time. They were the sore spots that your partner touched off almost accidentally. He probably didn't intend to hurt you. And even if he did, he must have had something in his past that hurt him or her so badly that he needed to hurt others. Once you see all that, you can opt for a beautiful reconciliation to take place.

You probably know what pushes your partner's buttons, what riles him up, but do you know what makes him happy? Do you know how to end the argument so that she feels content? When was the last time you went out of your way to make your partner happy or to do it his way? Practice doing the things that make your partner happy, and if you've forgotten what they might be, ask her, "How can we end this argument so that there are good feelings between us?"

Three steps toward reconciliation:

1. Be willing to be wrong. Not everything is worth being right about.

2. An apology can mean everything, so be sure to apologize when you've gone over the line. Be specific about what you are apologizing for.

3. Find the humor in your quarrels and be willing to laugh about your quirks.

 Examine the seeds of anger in yourself and you will understand that the person who has harmed you is suffering himself.

PART 3 In the Presence of Children

> In all situations, it is my response that decides whether
> a crisis will be escalated or de-escalated and a person
> humanized or dehumanized. If we treat people as
> they are, we make them worse. If we treat people as
> they ought to be, we help them become what they are
> capable of becoming.
>
> **—GOETHE**

Healthy family life allows for the civilized expression of anger. Children need the freedom to express anger *and* the safety of knowing that you as parent will not allow their behavior to get out of control. They need good guidance from a wise and centered parent.

Children get angry too. There's frequently a discrepancy between how we think our children ought to behave and how they actually do behave. We have ideals on the one hand and reality on the other. We think our children should conduct themselves in a respectful, polite manner, and they usually do, but they also get angry, scream, and throw temper tantrums occasionally too. Andy walked into the preschool to pick up four-year-old Luke and found him swearing and kicking the wall. The teachers were aghast; Andy was embarrassed. "How could you behave like that?" he asked, and then without waiting for an answer he grabbed Luke tightly by the arm and shoved him into the car.

When our children are mad and out of sorts, it's a challenge not to get angry ourselves. Anger is a call for help. When children are angry, they need you to set limits for their behavior while understanding the feelings that are causing the uproar. They need your help putting words to what they're feeling.

Children throw temper tantrums, sulk, pout, talk back, use dirty words, cry, fuss, hit, bite, are uncooperative, and act out. They have difficult moments and can be aggressive. When your kids are mad and behaving in ways you don't understand, you'll need all the parenting wisdom you can muster. Instead of yelling, "Stop it!" say, "Since we're both getting angry, let's count to ten." Then set the example by counting out loud. When your child is argumentative and shouting, you can firmly say, "We're mad now, so let's zip our lips and talk about it later."

More often than not, parents are as confused as children are about anger. As a parent, you must learn how to stay centered when the crankies overtake you. You *will* lose it; every parent does. Your kids will freak out and get angry, and so will you. But you both can begin again. You can teach safe ways for them to be angry and not get caught up in it. You won't succeed perfectly, but you'll make progress. You'll both be learning as you go along.

Remember, one part of anger relates to the situation at hand, the rest is internal and is a reaction to something else. Your kid had a tough day at kindergarten and is throwing a temper tantrum before he goes to bed. While it might be true that he doesn't want to go to bed right now, it's also true that he is bringing his past anger forward and working out his frustrations from school with you.

Acknowledge When Your Child Is Mad About Something

A cheerful four-year-old Abbey said to me one day, "I'm mad about something!"

"You're mad about something?" I repeated.

"Yup!" she said. "I'm mad, mad, mad about something."

"What made you so mad?" I asked.

"I don't know, I'm just mad."

What a relief, I thought to myself, to know that you're mad about something and can say it so proudly. Unfortunately, most children are not allowed to say how they're feeling. Many parents have trouble expressing anger themselves, and when their child is mad, the parents' confusion gets mixed in. Then, instead of getting mad and getting over it, they begin a commotion, and sadly, for some it continues for years. When a child is mad, accept it by saying, "You're mad!" and then show them that getting mad doesn't have to ruin the day.

Children of all ages and stages express anger. Every mother quickly learns to read the messages in her baby's cry. "He's mad that he has to go to bed, but he's so tired that he'll fall asleep in a couple of minutes," Libby explained about her ten-month-old.

Whether it's your two-year-old biting a playmate, your eight-year-old throwing his schoolbooks on the floor, or your teenager sulking and swearing, your child will demonstrate a wide range of frustrations. Children go through phases. When the adjustments they're making are difficult, they're likely to show anger and feel frustrated.

When your child is pouting, you can get the ball rolling in a positive direction by asking, "Are you mad that I didn't buy you that candy bar?" When your child is slamming the kitchen cupboards, you can avoid a tirade by biting your tongue and asking, "Are you mad that you have to do the dishes?" You'll avoid escalating his anger if you focus on one problem at a time. Instead of delivering a lecture, keep your comments sweet, short, and simple.

Labeling your child as angry because he's mad right now does nothing to help him cope with the feeling or modify his behavior. You never know for sure what sends a child over the edge. It could be that she's tired, still hurting from your divorce, upset about a friend at school, worried about the fight you and your husband are having, disturbed by something she saw on television, cranky that he can't understand a math problem. When you allow her to say, "I'm mad about something," you put a positive spin on what she's feeling. Sometimes the verbal expression of anger is all that's needed.

Set the example the next time you're stranded in traffic. Say in your best good-natured voice, "I mad about something," so that your kids in the back seat can hear. Then ask them if they can guess what that something is.

Teaching your child good anger management involves talking about mad feelings.

Be a Feeling Detective

Since kids don't have the emotional maturity to tell you when they're angry, hurt, sad, or lonely, you have to be a "feeling detective" to figure it out. Preverbal children cry and hit and use physical expression when they're angry, tired, or upset. Often when a child is restless, uncooperative, hitting, yelling, crying, bouncing up and down, swearing, or unable to sit still, that's an indication that the child either has needs that are being ignored or that he doesn't know how to handle what he's feeling. You might say, "It must have hurt your feelings terribly," or "You've been having a bad day," or "Something must have made you mad today."

Children need you to help them figure out what's going on inside themselves: "Are you upset that you couldn't go to the park today?"

When a child of any age is mad, he wants you to figure out what he's mad about. That's because he has a reason for feeling the way he does, and if someone at least understands he won't feel so alone. He'll be able to settle down because you listened. Upset teenagers need your undivided attention just as much as younger children do. Many anger problems escalate because of miscommunication or because the parent doesn't take the time to figure out what the child is feeling or thinking. A child needs you to validate that his feelings under the circumstances are normal. Then he needs your help finding a solution. The effort you make up-front to understand why your child is angry will save you lots of misunderstandings.

Once you've figured out what's bothering your child, never ridicule, make fun, or pooh-pooh her feelings. Instead of saying, "That's nothing to be upset about," or "Get over it," offer assistance: "Let's figure out how to make things better." Instead of, "That's no big deal," ask, "How can I help?"

Children need education to understand their feelings as much as they need education in any other subject. Not only are you the parent, you're the feeling detective, the coach, the advisor, the counselor, the educator.

 Children need your help in understanding and expressing their angry feelings.

Teach Talking versus Biting

Mothers often ask me what to do about a toddler's biting. Parents wonder if biting means that their child is headed in a negative direction. They worry that biting will become a habit. Biting is a phase, and while your child will outgrow it, she still needs attention and good guidance. She needs to learn to talk instead of biting.

If your child bites a playmate, the first thing to do is comfort the other child: "I'm sorry Hallie bit you; that was wrong. I know it hurts." That way you are letting the biter know that if she bites she won't get attention first. Next turn to the biter and calmly remove her from the situation. Give her a minute to relax. Sit on the floor at eye-to-eye level, gently put your hands on her shoulders, and say in a firm but friendly voice, "Don't bite. Biting hurts other people."

When twenty-one-month-old Derek bit his twin brother, his father bit Derek back. Glenn, the father, thought he was demonstrating that biting hurts, but I think he was teaching Derek that biting gets attention, and if Dad does it, it must be OK.

When a child is angry or upset, encourage her to use words instead of biting. Tell her to say, "I don't want to," or tell him it's OK to say "No." Let him know that he can always come to you for help to get his message across.

Helping your child manage her negative emotions begins very early. A toddler experiences a wide range of emotions. She's happy that she can play with the puzzle, but when she can't make the piece fit she gets mad and shows it in no uncertain terms. She needs your help to make sense of her feelings and learn how to control them. Toddlers understand when you talk to them about what they're feeling. When you talk to them you're giving them "talking tools." Then instead of biting, pulling, or shoving, they'll be more likely to say, "I'm mad, don't do that."

Most of a toddler's anger comes from frustration. They don't yet have the skills to communicate their wishes and wants. You have to do that for them. Saying "You're mad at the puzzle" labels the feeling so that she has words to describe what's going on inside. This helps her understand that what she feels is normal.

Toddlers have short attention spans, so when they're unhappy with what they're doing, give them something else to do. "Since you're mad at the puzzle, come play with the ball." You're labeling the feeling and giving them a constructive way to handle it.

As your child begins to learn the word *mad*, he'll be able to talk about what he's feeling. When you distract him, you teach him that when you're mad it's often more fun to walk away.

 If your toddler bites or hits, give them a one- to two-minute time out. Then tell them, "It's not OK to bite, it's not OK to hit."

Know That What You Say Does Matter

Banishing feelings makes them go underground. When you tell a child, "Don't feel that way," or "It's not nice to feel mad," the feeling doesn't go away, it gets hidden. Hidden anger gets disguised and often gathers momentum. It's easier to manage anger that's obvious than to redirect the hidden anger that comes out in roundabout ways.

When your child says, "My teacher is stupid," instead of saying, "Don't talk like that," ask, "What happened?" When he says, "My teacher made me stay in during recess," instead of saying, "Well, if you would have done your homework that wouldn't have happened," try, "That must have made you mad." The words you use when your child is expressing anger and frustration do matter. Your words teach compassion. Your child is learning to distinguish positive and negative emotions. By putting words to feelings, you're teaching him that feelings are normal and healthy. When your child is happy, notice that, and when your child is mad, notice that too. Don't scold her for feeling mad; empathize and you'll teach compassion.

When you help your children recognize their own feelings, you've laid the foundation for compassion. What you say and the tone in which you say it teaches your child how to treat others. You want your child to know that it's OK to feel mad, but it is not OK to hurt others.

You need to follow the same guidelines in your own behavior: It's OK for you to get mad at something your child is doing as long as you don't hurt her. A child learns empathy and compassion at home.

 Asking, "Did you have a bad day?" is better than asking, "What are you so mad about?"

Say "Yes" to Talking, "No" to Punching

No is a very important word in anger management. I am from the "encouragement school of parenting," which means that I think that children need encouragement more than discouragement. They need to hear, "Yes, you can," more than "No, you can't." Guiding them along by being generous with encouragement lets them feel positive about life and their ability to face frustrations. Children need plenty of "Yes" for sure, but they also need "No's" sprinkled in.

Destructive behavior and violence is a definite no-no. Tell them, "If you punch your brother, it hurts your brother and that is not allowed," or "It's OK to tell me that you're mad, but it is not OK to smash your toys."

Imposing hundreds of rules governing every little move your child makes creates a home life filled with tension. Rather than adding to the confusion, keep the rules simple. When you're mad you can't hurt things or people. You can talk with me about it, you can talk to your sister, but I won't allow you to hurt each other.

New frustrations come with every new developmental stage. A child at two may pull his playmate's hair, but if you tell him, "No," he'll learn that pulling hair is hurtful and won't be tolerated. Say "Yes" to talking, say "No" to punching, pinching, and hurting. If he learns that when he's young, he'll remember it as he grows.

Now here comes the really hard part. If you don't allow destructive, hurtful behavior, do you expose your children to it in your behavior? Do you hurt them? Do you tell them not to hit, and then turn around and hit them? Do you tell them not to slap each other, but do you sometimes slap them? Do you spank your children?

Six-year-old Molly played with the dollhouse and miniature dolls in my office. The mommy and daddy doll spanked the child doll; the child doll spanked the baby. "Does the baby spank?" I asked. "The baby is too little to spank," Molly answered. Molly was spanked by both her parents. They told me that since they were both spanked as children, that's what they did with Molly. Molly was a sensitive little girl; since she was pulling out her hair and biting her nails until they bled, her parents were beginning to wonder whether spanking was an effective discipline.

What you do and what you say need to match. If hitting is not allowed in your family, don't hit children. If you do hit your children, they will probably at some time or another hit another child or strike out in the way they learned from you.

Any chronic destructive behavior your child displays, such as biting, talking back, hitting, or an obstinate disposition, indicates that your child is going through a difficult adjustment—a new baby brother, a move, learning a new skill. It's a signal that he is in grave need of extra attention and guidance from you.

 You child learns about his own anger by watching how *you* manage anger. Ways of handling anger are to suppress it, talk about it, throw fits, get violent, and get physical exercise. Which ways do you want your child to learn?

Recognize the Spectrum of Anger

From a two-year-old who has a temper tantrum because he didn't want to sit in the car seat to the defiant child who actively disobeys you and deliberately picks on his schoolmates, children display a wide spectrum of anger. Children get angry for all the reasons that adults get angry—fear, loneliness, disappointment, stress, and hurt. Girls and boys in our society learn to express their dissatisfactions and frustrations differently. Girls are told that "nice" girls don't get mad, so instead of expressing anger they say, "You hurt my feelings," or they might cry. Girls in general are more indirect; they communicate hostility toward peers by manipulation. Cliques of teenage girls are known for handling their upsets by spreading rumors.

Boys learn that it's not okay to cry, so instead of shedding tears when they're hurt, they might punch the wall or start a fight. Boys confront each other directly and use verbal assaults.

Like adults, both boys and girls have trouble identifying anger when they feel it and difficulty releasing it appropriately once it's felt.

Three-year-old Riley is tired from a full day at the amusement park, and when she comes home she throws herself on the floor and wails, "I want my teddy." Eight-year-old Melanie is disappointed that her best friend got sick and can't spend the night. She's cranky and slams the door; she lies on her bed and won't eat dinner. Ten-year-old Zach lost his favorite baseball mitt; when his seven-year-old brother walks by he throws a book at him. When his mom comes to see what all the commotion is about, he yells at her to "get out of my room!" After her parents separated, fifteen-year-old Sarah began missing classes because she couldn't get up in the morning. Her grades plummeted and she complained, "I don't have any friends." Sixteen-year-old Mitch is surly to every adult he comes in contact with and has decided he no longer has to abide by curfew.

When I talk with children and parents about anger, I divide anger into three categories. By understanding the different degrees of anger, parents can have clearer ideas of what interventions might be needed.

1. Little Anger: Little anger is momentary and specific. For example, five-year-old Jake didn't get a second ice cream cone

so he's pouting; ten-year-old Adam swore when he struck out in the baseball game. Little angers are easily solved and vanish with understanding. Make a clear statement of your standards: "You're disappointed because you struck out, but no swearing allowed on the field."

2. Big Anger: Big anger is intense and covers up low self-esteem and self-doubt. It's often disguised as depression and is a symptom of an underlying problem that needs attention. Big anger is often related to trauma, grief, or loss. Eleven-year-old Amy refuses to join any after-school activities because "the kids at my school are stupid." By the fourth grade, Max was fighting on the school grounds and was known as the neighborhood bully. A child with a big anger is unhappy and needs intervention and guidance to heal the wound that is causing the problem.

3. Huge Anger: Huge anger is rage, a profound and uncontrollable feeling in the body, almost on the cellular level, of wanting to hurt yourself or someone else. Rage results from emotional abandonment, abuse by parents, or repeated alienation from peers. As an infant Justin was physically abused by his mother and abandoned by his alcoholic father. At fourteen years old, he's defiant, skipping school, and drinking. Rage can also arise from repeated rejection by peers. By the eighth grade, Allison had gone to four different schools. She was bashful, and each new school felt like one more rejection to her. It was hard to make friends, so she put on a tough exterior and acted as if she didn't care.

Huge anger causes many problems for the child and for those around him. A child with such a deep wound is living in a state of emergency. He needs immediate and daily assistance to overcome his hurt and rage. He needs strong limits on his destructive behavior and skill-building for competent behaviors.

Chalking anger up to a stage that your child is going through is not a good approach. While it's true that two-years-olds grow out of grabbing toys from their playmates, they still need your guidance to figure out what to do in social situations. Even though you know that this is not the last boyfriend your teenage daughter will have, when she's crying because he broke up with her and calling herself names for liking him in the first place, she still needs you to understand the agony she's feeling. She needs your support as she finds ways to get through her heartache rather than letting the rejection define her. A teenager will probably outgrow his tendency to shrug you off when you ask about his day, but in the meantime he needs you to stay connected. If you ignore him altogether he wonders why you don't seem to care anymore, and although he may never tell you, he definitely feels abandoned.

There is a difference between angry feelings and angry acts, and they need to be handled differently. Angry feelings need to be identified and expressed. Angry acts need to be restricted and redirected.

Teaching good anger management to children usually involves both parts—allowing the expression of angry feelings while limiting angry behavior. Sometimes it's sufficient simply to identify a child's feeling, but when the child is acting in destructive ways, appropriate limits need to be set. When seven-year-old Alexis slammed the door, her mother said, "Come tell me what you're mad about." But when Alexis kicked the cat, her mother stepped in and said, "I know you're upset that you can't play outside in the rain, but you can't take it out on the cat. Go get a book and we can read a story." She acknowledged the feeling, limited the behavior, and redirected the energy toward something positive.

Good anger management is educational in nature. It preserves the child's self-respect by acknowledging his feelings and inner conflicts, and then channels inappropriate behaviors into creative, constructive activities.

 Anger comes in degrees: *Little Anger* is momentary and specific; *Big Anger* is intense and covers up feelings of depression and low self-esteem; *Huge Anger* is rage and covers up deep emotional wounds.

Stop the Ripple Effect

A family behaves like a unit. If one person is angry, you can bet the others feel it. When one member of your family is sad or afraid, there's a ripple affect, like dropping a peddle into a pond. All the family members are touched. If the parents are angry at each other, the children feel that. If the siblings are fighting and mad at each other, the parents are affected. An anger problem in the family means everyone is suffering.

A child with a huge anger needs help, and so does the family. You can't expect things to get better if you treat only the child. Family members are like the tires on a car: without one tire, the car doesn't operate. Just as the four tires work in unison, each member has an important part in the operation of the family. If you're child is angry, obstinate, full of rage and anger, you're affected, and everyone will need new strategies. You can't just drop the child off at a counselor's office and expect things to get better. You're needed there too.

A family is a joint system. If the parents are unhappy in their marriage, the child will sense that and be affected by it. If the parents disagree yet try to present a united front, the child will know it and may get mixed messages. A child is seriously affected when one parent disparages the other. Parents sometimes put the child in the middle of marital arguments; instead of dealing with the hostility, hurt, and disappointment that's between them they unknowingly direct it through the child. Then the child acts out. What really is going on is that the child's behavior reflects unclear messages and parents' unresolved issues.

For the sake of your family, if there is an anger problem with any member, gather everybody up and go for counseling. The whole family thrives when one angry member is loved and supported by the others. Making the time to love the child who is hurt, fearful, or angry by getting him the help that he needs is worth it, because all the family members benefit.

 When one member of your family is angry, sad, afraid, mad, hurt, or in pain, all the family members feel it.

Remove Harmful Shame

Shame causes all of us—children and adults alike—to hide. We feel as though we've been stupid or done something revolting—failed in some unfathomable way. What you considered private was publicly ridiculed. And the memory of how we were exposed still haunts us, still makes us squirm. You liked someone and when that was discovered, you were ridiculed for it. You made a mistake and everybody laughed.

When you understand how shame shrinks and shrivels you, you will never use shame to get your child to behave. You will understand that shame breeds the most violent of thoughts and deeds. Shame causes a child to feel blemished, defective in the most grotesque way. Children who suffer from shame say terrible things to themselves: I'm worthless, I'm awful, I can't do anything right, I don't deserve to be alive.

A ten-year-old boy was referred to me for counseling by the school psychologist for being defiant and oppositional. We worked for almost a year together before he trusted me with a very difficult story about the times he kicked his dog. He felt such intense shame and remorse that it affected his life and he believed himself to be a "bad seed." He vowed he would never do it again, but he couldn't stop himself. He felt angry, but he didn't know why. He didn't know why he did it—it was a strong uncontrollable urge. He put his head on the table and cried. He was inconsolable.

His mother had used shame to get him to mind. She pointed her left index finger at him and rubbed her right index finger over it and mockingly said, "Shame on you!" whenever he messed up. She poked fun and called him wimpy when he cried. She criticized him in front of others, and when he wet the bed, she told his sister, "Look at the big baby."

Lest you think the mother was a bad person, I want you to know that she was not. As a child, she was not only shamed herself, she was beaten. She desperately wanted to stop the legacy of abuse that she'd lived under, so she never once beat her son. She loved him, wanted the best for him, but it wasn't until she reached out and came for counseling that she understood the legacy of shame that she and her son lived under.

I worked with this family for three years, and the results renewed my faith in grace, redemption, and the beautiful spirit that lies within us all. Mother and son learned the effect of their shaming words and stopped using them. When she had a complaint with him, she took him aside and spoke with him respectfully. The mother started noticing when her son was doing something right, and she gave him recognition for it. She admired his determination and she told him so.

With his mother's admiration behind him, instead of mouthing off, arguing, and defying her, the boy learned more effective ways to fight for his rights. Instead of trying to prove people wrong, he learned how to treat people fairly. At age fourteen, the son was awarded a plaque at school assembly for being the student who had made the most improvement. This boy who once had no friends was given a standing ovation by the student body.

As this story illustrates, it is never too late to change. It is never too late to learn a new behavior, to find a way to help your child. No matter what you're situation is, you can make it better.

 Shame causes a child to hate himself. When a child hates himself, he becomes very angry and lashes out in violent ways.

Deal with Your Child Directly

Eleven-year-old Jade walked into the kitchen and announced, "I'm in a bad mood today!" and grabbed the cereal box out of her brother's hands. "It's OK to be in a bad mood, but it's not OK to take it out on us," her father firmly reminded her.

While I advocate treating your child kindly, I also advocate putting your foot down when necessary to let your child know that you're the parent. I advocate firmness *and* kindness. All children test their parents, and that's perfectly normal. It's part of the process of growing up. Likewise, every parent knows that while you can overlook many behaviors and moods, there are times when you have to put your foot down and reestablish your parental authority.

Carter is a freckled-faced, blonde, mouthy little kid. He is curious, cute, and smart. He rules his parents and runs circles around his teachers. When his parents try to punish him, he has temper tantrums that last for hours. One night after three hours of battling failed to get Carter to complete his fifteen minutes of homework, the father gave up and called the police. The police came to the house and gave Carter a lecture, and he calmed right down. But as soon as the police left Carter was screaming obscenities.

The second time I saw Carter in my office he started banging his legs against the wall. He looked at me as if testing me to see what I would do. The parents looked to see what I would do. I looked directly at Carter and said, "Knock it off!" and he did immediately. I'd established my authority and he responded to it. Now his parents had to reclaim their authority. They had to deal directly with their child because it was ridiculous to call in the militia every night to get an eight-year-old to do his homework.

A child must live by your rules. Your rules need to be flexible enough to allow for individual needs, developmental levels, learning curves, bad times, and the child's progress. Taking all that into consideration, a child who refuses day after day, night after night to abide by common decency needs you to step in and reestablish who's boss.

You do that by using the leverage you have. To reestablish their authority, Carter's parents had to take away all his perks. That meant no computer, TV, root beer floats, Game Boy, or allowance. If he didn't go by the rules, his life was going to be miserable. The parents continued to do this until Carter got the idea, stopped with the tantrums, and started doing his homework.

You are the boss, the parent, the chairman of the board. Don't flaunt it, but don't ever forget it.

 When your child is out of control and running the show, you need to reestablish your parental authority by putting your foot down.

Listen to Your Child's Complaints

When I see kids in my office who are angry and upset, I invite them to talk with me about it. "You seem upset today," I say, and then I pause, giving them time to respond. Some kids are quite verbal and begin recounting all the details about what's bothering them. Others nod and struggle to find the words. But regardless of how they begin and regardless of their age—whether they're eight or eighteen—there's a similar theme in what they express. Amidst their individual concerns is the viewpoint that "my parents don't believe me," or "they're too busy to listen to what I'm saying," or "my parents don't care," or "my parents don't know who I am." "My parents don't listen" is their number one complaint.

Fifteen-year-old Allison complained, "My mom grounded me for one whole month for coming home forty-five minutes late."

"You're very upset," I said.

"Now I don't get to go to the ninth grade dance," she answered.

"You're disappointed," I said.

"My mother gives into my brother, but not to me. She grounded Sean," Allison explained, "but he still got to go to his football games and the awards banquet."

"Oh," I said.

"Mom says my situation is different," replied Allison, "but she always gives into to Sean. He's her favorite."

"Have you considered talking to her about this?" I asked.

"She won't listen," Allison said.

Allison wants her mother's attention and goes to great lengths to get it. She's dyed her hair purple, which her mother hates, and cut holes in her brand new jeans. She sneaks out at night, she slides by at school. She's mouthy one minute—"Whatever," she smirks—and then she cooperates the next—"I take off my shoes just like Mom wants me to whenever I walk on her carpet."

"Your daughter is trying to tell you something," I tell the mom. She shrugs and says, "Allison has always thought I like Sean best, but it's just not true." Allison and Mom are defensive, locked in a "Yes, you do; No, I don't" debate.

Painful and angry feelings are wrapped up with complaints. If you're finding it difficult to listen to your child's complaints, perhaps it's because it's hard to listen to the pain your child is feeling. Or perhaps you think that the pain means that you are a bad parent. All parent-child relationships have difficulties; the successful ones deal with the pain and anger.

When parents jump in quickly to defend themselves, explain, or fix the problem, they end up not only dismissing the complaint, but also the anger and hurt that comes with it. You miss the opportunity to address the real issues; the conclusion that your child frequently comes to is that "my parents don't listen," or "my parents don't care." Complaints that aren't heard don't go away, they grow larger and are often acted out in more harmful ways.

When your child is behaving in ways that you don't understand, it usually means he is trying to get your attention, to tell you something. Listening to your child's complaints requires maturity on your part because some of the criticism may be about you. Even it the criticism is irrational, you have to hear your child out in order to get to the bottom of what's troubling her. A child who is ignored either buries her concerns or turns to someone else.

 Welcome your child's complaints and solve them together. Tell him, "Thank you for bringing this to my attention. I'm glad we can negotiate."

First Give Understanding

Nothing diffuses a child's anger better than an understanding parent. Anger loses its sharp edges when you simply accept it. Your understanding forms a basis for the child's learning how to express anger; it frees the child to share what happened and how he felt. Without someone to understand, a child is overwhelmed by her feelings, with no idea how to figure out what's bothering her. Lisa told her eight-year-old son, "Whenever you're feeling angry, come to me and I will stop whatever I'm doing to listen to your concerns. I will help you plan what you can do so that you won't stay mad."

Every child is entitled to be angry, and every child needs good guidance to learn how to deal with anger effectively. By respectfully responding to your child's angry feelings, you're paving the way for the instruction that you may need to give and for the limits that you'll need to set.

A child caught up in all those angry feelings is not thinking clearly; he's mad and showing it. What he needs from you is attentive understanding, recognizing what is going on inside him at the particular moment. Let your child know that you're on her side by saying something like, "Wow! You sound angry," or "You must be disappointed that you didn't make the team," or "That must be frustrating for you." Statements of understanding such as, "I see," "What happened next?" "You must have been upset," invite continued conversation, which then paves the way for problem solving.

Fourteen-year-old Lauren says, "My mother likes my sister Allie best." Lora rebuts, "Now Lauren that's not true; Allie gets away with more because she's younger than you," which leads to more arguing between them. When Mom stopped defending and said, "Help me understand what you mean," the tension dissolved between them.

When your child believes that you understand what he is mad about, his anger dissolves and he feels less alone. Letting her know that her feelings are acceptable calms her frustrations.

Statements of understanding always come before giving advice, asking questions, or setting limits.

Respond to "I Hate You"

If your child has ever screamed at you, "I hate you!" you know how those three words can pierce your heart. If you're like most parents, hearing that come out of your darling's mouth can cause you to wonder where you went wrong. Some parents hear those words and scream right back.

When Stephanie told her seven-year-old son he had to come in for dinner, he screamed, "I hate you, I hate you." She was appalled at what she considered his disrespectful behavior and shouted back, "Don't talk to me like that," and sent him to his room. "Now stay there until you straighten up."

A child's screaming "I hate you!" is not a reflection of your parenting skills, but rather an expression of the anger your child is feeling for not getting his way or for not being understood. If you snap back in anger, that doesn't help the situation. "I know you want to play outside, and I can understand why you're angry, but dinner is ready and you have to come in." Then add, "Take a time out and when you've cooled down, come eat dinner."

If hearing "I hate you" upsets you, it's best to talk about it after the frenzy of the moment has passed. The next day, in a friendly, upbeat manner you might say, "I understand that you were mad at me yesterday when you said, 'I hate you,' but in our family we don't talk like that because it's hurtful."

Anger doesn't disappear just because you tell a child, "It's not nice to feel that way," or "You shouldn't feel that way." Marne told me, "My father would say, 'Don't talk to us like that,' and I learned quickly that if I continued to talk that way that I'd get in trouble. I stopped, but it didn't stop me from thinking and feeling." Anger diminishes and loses its intensity when you accept the feelings. Then you can make the guidelines for behavior perfectly clear because your child will more likely be listening.

Fantasizing about how much you hate your parents is normal. Being mad is all right as long as you don't try to justify temporary feelings of hate with some philosophy or ideology. It's only when we hold onto our hatred by justifying it that danger arises. In my home, my counseling, and my workshops, participants don't ever give reasons for feeling what they feel. We just feel whatever we feel and we know that's OK. Nobody says, "How dare you," or "You shouldn't." Anger, hate, detesting, disliking—as long as they are just feelings—open the way to love. But if you justify hate by saying, "I hate this person because . . ."—because their skin is a certain color, or because they believe such and such—then you're in trouble. The real haters buttress their hate with some kind of philosophy.

A child will occasionally say, "I hate you!" but that doesn't mean that they hate you. Maybe they would like to hate you, maybe they think they hate you, maybe they're mad at what you're doing, but more likely what they're really feeling are outrage and the humiliation of being small and helpless.

 If hearing your child say "I hate you" upsets you, give her another way that she can let you know when she is frustrated or angry with you.

Stay Close

Loneliness can be one cause for prickly, argumentative behavior. When a child screams, "Leave me alone!" either with words or with actions, it may be a sign of how badly he's hurting. When your child is behaving in ways that you don't understand, always look deeper than what you can see on the surface. If your child says, "Leave me alone," and they bounce back feeling happy when you do, the downtime was what they needed. But if they are not refreshed by being left alone, then that's a signal that they're really longing for *more* connection, not less.

One of the biggest hurts for a preteen and teenager is social isolation. Diane knew that her eleven-year-old daughter, Maddy, was having a difficult adjustment to her new school. She didn't like it that Maddy was spending all her free time alone in her room, but whenever she made suggestions, Maddy snapped, "I don't want to talk about it." Discouraged and not knowing what to do next, Diane decided, "She'll probably grow out of it." Five years later, when they were fighting daily, they came for counseling. Maddy was talking on the phone all night and occasionally sneaking out to be with friends. When Diane understood the depth of loneliness that Maddy still felt, she was able to put the behavior in perspective. Instead of labeling Maddy a rebellious teenager and leaving it at that, Diane responded to the loneliness that still lingered. Once Diane understood Maddy's longing for friendship, they negotiated telephone hours and a curfew that would allow Maddy ample time for socializing and for Diane to feel comfortable too.

Children need opportunities to make friends. Teens report that it's often more difficult to make friends in junior high than in grade school. If you sense that your child is having difficulty making friends, guide him toward activities where he might meet other students with similar interests. Encourage after-school activities and team participation. Invite your child's friends to your home; occasionally include your child's friend on a family outing.

Parents frequently ask me what to do if they don't like one of their child's friends. My advice is that unless the friend is involved in drugs or alcoholic or illegal activities, it's best to allow the contact to continue. If they really don't have anything in common, it's likely that they will go their separate ways soon. Be grateful that your child has someone she can talk with.

Angry, aggressive kids are often scolded for being upset, then left to their own devices. Closing your heart and shutting down when your children are being naughty, angry, mad, and disrespectful leaves them even more isolated and abandoned. This is the time to stay open and be absolutely available. It's no big deal to stay close to a perfect child who is doing everything exactly as you wish, but the ability to give understanding to a child who is upset or not cooperating with you is what separates the real parents from the fakes.

Remember, when your daughter or son is wearing a prickly shield, instead of putting on a matching one, take your guard down and say, "Honey, I'm concerned that you're spending too much time alone. Can we talk about it?" And even if they bristle at your offer, don't let it drop too quickly. Bring it up again.

 When your child says, "Leave me alone," pay attention. If everything is going well in her life, some time alone is normal, but if this becomes a regular pattern, you must investigate further.

Acknowledge Grief

Some children put on an aloof and angry demeanor when they're grieving. Sadness can often appear as a gloomy, hostile, "Don't bug me!" attitude. Children and teenagers grieve the losses in their lives too. The death of grandparent, a pet dying, a playmate moving, a move to a new school, a parents' divorce, a breakup with a boyfriend, all are significant losses for your child or teen. Some children withdraw when they suffer a loss and will not let themselves get close. They fear being hurt again. They're more irritable and snappy. They appear cranky and sullen. Unresolved grief often leads to destructive relationships with adults, especially if the adult does not recognize the grief underneath the crabby, angry demeanor.

Children do grieve. They're society's "forgotten mourners." Their feelings are as intense, as real as any grieving adult's. When a child is hurt, lonely, suffering, or grieving, he often appears to have a chip on his shoulder. This is when your child is the most vulnerable. Perhaps he's worried that something bad will happen to you or others that he cares about. When someone she loves gets hurt or dies, the notion of "It can't happen to me" is smashed, and she begins thinking, "It happened once; it can happen again." Here again you have to be the feeling detective, to figure out what's going on so that you can respond with kindness and appropriate interventions.

Whether it's the loss of an acquaintance, a close friend, a relative, or a pet, show compassion for the loss by giving extra tender loving care. Comfort him and make allowances for sullen looks and short answers. Acknowledge the loss: "I'm so sorry your friend moved away. You must miss her very much." Ignore the surliness, pay attention to the ache: "You're having a difficult time since we moved so far away. I'm sorry you're feeling so lonely."

Bereaved children may show anger both at the person they lost and at you. Don't fault them for that. It's a natural response. When a death occurs, your child may "strike out," not knowing what to do with his anger. When there is no understanding of the grief process and no safe place to vent feelings of pain and confusion, violent or reckless behavior may occur. Unexpressed grief can lead to a lifetime of undefined depression.

Children need significant support as they deal with loss. They are often pressured "to put it behind them" and "move on," when what they really need is to process the loss by remembering and talking. The key to healthy grieving is open communication within the family and the support of a social network. Let your child know that you care and that you are willing to talk openly about what has happened. Make sure the school knows what has happened and keep communication open with them.

A child who is given the opportunity to process her feelings of loss will feel empowered with the tools to handle the losses that continue to occur throughout life. Just as you tell your child that it is okay to be sad sometimes and cry, tell him too that it is definitely okay to feel angry and be mad sometimes.

Some children need quiet downtime to recover from a loss, and you can allow this as long as the connection with you is stable. You don't always have to be cheering them up or keeping them busy, but you do have to let them know how much you care. Stay connected, watch closely, and make sure they get what they need to heal.

Children need to know that *you* are okay. Often, children "protect" the adults around them, at great cost to their own emotional needs. If you are grieving too and cannot attend to your child's needs right now, ask another reliable adult who can respond for help.

 A child who is behaving in negative ways may be dealing with a significant loss.

Throw Rocks in Water, Throw a Ball, Play Kick the Can

Physical activity helps when you're mad or are having a bad day. Kids can release considerable pent-up energy through play and exercise. Skipping rocks across water and watching the ripples is soothing. Throwing a ball and kicking a can around calms you down. When Claudia gets mad at her stepmother, Dad takes her to hit a bucket of balls at the driving range. On the way home they stop for a treat and talk about what's going on at home.

There's considerable debate on anger theory and the value of catharsis. Some experts think that expressing anger by hitting a punching bag, pounding a pillow with a bat, or taking your aggression out on an inanimate object is a healthy way to vent. Some studies, however, suggest that unless a child has an adult to guide them through the thinking process, hitting and punching is likely to end up making things worse. In my experience, children need a combination of physical activity, understanding, and problem-solving skills. They need you to coach them.

A client of mine, newly widowed with a twelve-year-old daughter, decided that to move through the pain they needed to participate in a physical activity together. Although she wasn't sure she had the energy, she signed them up for horse riding lessons. After each class they went out to dinner. This weekly physical activity and dinner ritual made it possible for her daughter to talk about how much she missed her Dad.

I like the outdoor game of Kick the Can as an anger-reducing exercise; it's better than computer games for soothing anger. Computer games heighten arousal, making anger control problems worse. Team sports have their place, but in some cases the pressure of competition leads to more frustration and aggression. When you're mad, kicking a can around outside can reconnect you to your spirit.

Understanding + Physical Activity + Coaching = Anger Mastery.

Hammer Nails

If you've ever pounded a nail or used a hammer, you know the thrill of accomplishment that comes with funneling anger and energy into a creative building project. After experiencing a business failure, a neighbor of mine built an entire addition onto his house with the help of his eleven-year-old daughter. Hammering nails is a constructive way to handle anger and disappointment.

The thrill of accomplishment that comes with venting anger in productive ways is more satisfying than the low that comes with seeking revenge. Beating up on your pillow may bring momentary relief, but when you're done, except for the feathers flying, you don't have anything to show for all that commotion. Tearing the pages from a telephone book is better than taking your animosities out on each other, but I'm not sure that any good lessons come from even minor destruction.

Physical releases of anger are best when channeled into creative outlets. My client, Juliet, a mother of two, designed and built a deck onto her little cottage after her husband left. Her twelve-year-old daughter and sixteen-year-old son were very angry at their father too, but since Juliet didn't want to reinforce the hatred they were all feeling, "I bit my tongue and built the deck," she said. "It's my policy that if I can't say anything nice, I do something constructive." All summer the kids watched as Juliet sawed, hammered, and step by step built the deck. By the time the deck was complete, Juliet said, "I was still hurt, but I wasn't so mad anymore. I'm worn out but proud of how well we're all moving on."

Instead of saying, "Don't get mad," say, "Let's do something constructive." And then give the kids a hammer or some paintbrushes. Build a birdhouse, paint the bedroom, build a fence.

 A healthy antidote for anger is a creative project done together.

Paint a Mad Picture

Painting a mad picture is a creative way to help children think over what they're feeling. This works wonders for small children who don't have the skills to verbalize what's going on and for anyone who has been taught that expressing anger is some kind of sin. Sometimes you can put it on paper better than you can say it.

Make sure you have a large box of color crayons on hand. And when you or your child is frustrated, just start drawing or scribbling away. Don't plan it out; just let your unconscious do the work. It's almost like dreaming. After you're done you can look at your pictures and see what you've come up with.

Mad pictures sometimes look scary, but don't worry. It's just your unconscious mind ridding itself of the demons that have been haunting you. Scribbling in a journal helps relieves stress too. Writing or drawing about a stressful experience reduces tensions and fears.

Kate, the mother, and thirteen-year-old Lyndsey were locked in a name-calling battle. "I'm so mad at my mom I won't ever do what she wants again," Lyndsey told me. "I'm so mad at her she can go live with her dad," Kate said. I tried to help them talk about it, but when it was clear that wouldn't work, I asked them to draw how mad they were, then talk about the pictures. Lyndsey drew a red-faced monster and said, "That's Mom!" Kate drew a monster too and said, "No! That's you!" They laughed and agreed that they were both like monsters when they're mad.

Drawing mad pictures together works because children are longing for their parents' undivided attention. I know that this seems impossible for many parents who are already overwhelmed. But kids tell me they want more time to hang out with their parents. Teens tell me, "I wish my parents would listen more."

In any stressful situation, ask yourself,

What does my child need?

What is he trying to tell me?

If I were this child, how would I want to be treated?

Is he hungry?

Does he need something to drink, unwinding time, do-nothing time, time to relax, or sleep?

Is he bored?

Does he need an activity, a hobby, a sport?

Does he need attention, acknowledgment, and praise?

Does he need a routine, consistency, and limits?

Does he need a hug, individual attention?

Does he need some good listening or comforting?

Does he need help solving a problem?

Does he need freedom?

Does he need to feel safe?

Does he need a dose of laughter?

 Draw pictures together to help your child express anger in a healthy way.

Be Smarter Than the Bullies

If your child is a bully, it's because he's trying to make himself feel better; if he's being bullied, he needs to learn how to handle the bullies. A bully uses his anger to hurt others; the kid who copes with the bully uses anger effectively to empower himself.

My friend Bob told me this story: "My most positive experience was at age thirteen when I got mad and completely lost my temper. After years of being bullied in school, I used all my anger and energy to settle the matter once and for all. I beat up and threw the person who was making my life miserable down a flight of stairs. Life became quite nice for me after that, but I don't think this is something you would want to talk about in your book." Well, sometimes you do what you have to do.

There are always bullies around, and your kids will have to deal with them. They'll need backup and training from you to do that. The first step is to help your child understand the bully mentality. Bullies take pleasure out of making someone else feel inferior.

The best approach is, Give a bully as little ammunition as possible. It's best not to talk back because a bully is usually better with put-downs and smart remarks. Your child may have already tried the "avoid the bully " tactic and may need other strategies as well. Your role is to coach your child as she develops the inner strength to resolve her conflicts.

The kid's in Michelle's neighborhood treated her badly. Michelle's mother said, "Those kids are brats," which really wasn't helpful. That only perpetuated Michelle's lack of confidence and didn't give her any useful tactics. Michelle decided that karate might do the trick. She never used it on the bullies in her neighborhood, but she felt empowered. It gave her a boost in confidence.

Whenever you witness a child being picked on or bullied, you as the adult must not allow it. You must investigate the incident, find the cause, and enforce a solution that satisfies both parties.

Most children who hit, yank, and punch other children have been hit and spanked at home. All little bullies have been beaten on by a big parental bully.

Coach and Check Back

Telling your child that she can come to you if she ever needs help is a good message, but it's not enough. To become proficient in any skill, including anger management, a child needs a daily dose of coaching. Twelve-year-old Nick got into a bloody fistfight with another boy during the school lunch break. His parents were called for a conference. Both boys were brought in and told that if they hit each other again they'd be suspended. The principal said that in the future, rather than fighting it out, the boys should come to the office to talk it out.

The parents agreed with the plan, but wisely they took it one step further. Joe told his son Nick, "I'll check with you tomorrow to see how your day goes," and he did. In fact he checked back with Nick at the end of every school day for the next four months. "How did things go at school today?" he asked, or he'd say, "What's up?" Joe listened carefully to find out what Nick was having trouble handling. He coached Nick on anger management, and then like a good coach he stepped back and let Nick handle it. "If you need me to step in I will, but I think you can handle it. It's OK to get angry, but if you hit each other you'll get kicked out of school. Getting kicked out of school is not acceptable to me. Other solutions are better."

Anger management coaching is not the same as lecturing. Good coaching is developing a game plan with the player, making sure that the rules are being followed, allowing for errors, and plenty of pep talks. Good coaching is not a one-time effort; it's daily or weekly involvement that allows for the change of bad habits and for gaining capability. By the time Joe was through coaching, Nick incorporated the game plan so well that he memorized it.

Here's the game plan:

1. Stop and chill: When you're mad about something, stop! Chill out. Take a walk, get a drink of water, and cool down. Don't be a fool; act cool!

2. Think smart: Think. Think. Think! What's the *smart* thing to do? Don't be dumb; be smart. Don't do something stupid. If you're going to do something—do something smart.

3. Talk it out: Can you talk to the person you're angry with?

Can you talk it over with someone else? When you talk directly to the other person, it works best to say, "Can we talk?" then begin with, "Can we work this out?" Listen carefully to what the other person says. Maybe you can find a solution. If you can't talk about it to the other party, talk to someone else.

Walking away, cooling down, and talking is not being a "chicken"; it's a strategic action.

 Instead of leaving kids to "fight it out," we need to teach them to "talk it out."

Take Five Steps to a Face-Saving Dialogue

For your child to maintain her self-respect, it's important for her to be able to save face. If you're mad at your child about something, shaming him magnifies the problem. Not only will he feel bad for messing up, he'll feel demoralized and come to the self-defeating conclusion that he is a bad person. If you consider your child to be wrong, pointing it out again and again won't get you anyplace. Humiliating doesn't work; shaming doesn't work. Grounding and restriction aren't effective unless you include a Face-Saving Dialogue.

A face-saving dialogue shows respect and motivates your child to do better. Children don't want to let their parents down, and when you have a face-saving dialogue you show them that while you're disappointed and mad that they goofed up, you still believe that they will do better the next time.

Five Steps to a Face-Saving Dialogue

1. Acknowledge the anger: "I'm mad that you went to the concert without my permission."

2. Acknowledge the hurt: "I'm disappointed because I thought we had an agreement."

3. Acknowledge the fear: "I'm afraid when you don't come home on time."

4. Acknowledge the love: "I appreciate you talking with me about this. I want us to cooperate and find a better solution for next time."

5. Acknowledge your part: "I'm sorry that I yelled last night, I know that made it worse."

Your children look up to you; you set the example. When you have face-saving dialogues with your children, they'll learn the steps. Eventually, when they are mad at you about something, they'll have a face-saving dialogue with you.

A face saving dialogue is getting the information across without putting your child down.

Be Aware That Children Are Watching

Have you heard the cries of a baby startled by his parents' loud angry voices? Have you noticed the look in your child's eyes when you're angry and taking it out on him? If you've ever seen the look on a child's face as he hears his parents calling each other names, if you've ever seen the sadness in the eyes of a child whose parents are pushing and shoving, you know the toll such hostility can take on their souls.

Anger frightens children. It affects learning, self-esteem, and overall happiness. Living with anger makes children nervous. They can't remember or learn when they're frightened; they can't relax or think clearly. They wonder what they've done wrong. All their energies go into avoiding trouble. Imagine what it must feel like to be small and have a giant of a parent, someone you admire and trust, standing over you with a gnarly, angry face, yelling at you. Yelling "You're so stupid" doesn't make them smart. Angry shouting may get a child to mind, but it slowly erodes any comfort in your alliance.

"I yelled at my daughter, 'Why can't you pick up your backpack and shoes?' I really lost it," Paul told me. "My daughter looked at me and said, 'Well Dad, if you ask me nicely, a least when I get around to doing it, I'd be more cheerful about it.'" Asking a child ten times, "Will you please take out the garbage?" is exasperating. No wonder parents come to the conclusion that yelling is the only way to get things done. I've done it myself, but each time I yelled to get things done, I was left with a gnawing ache inside, because I knew that asking nicely ten times was a better example to set for my daughter than yelling and getting angry.

Six-year-old Jake told me, "I get so mad when my stepsister swears at me that I want to say swear words back at her, but my mom won't let me because I'm too little."

"How do you keep yourself from swearing when you're so mad?" I asked.

"I remember that I'm not suppose to swear and I don't do it."

Jake exercised a degree of self-control that even his father, mother, stepmother, stepfather, older half-siblings, and stepsiblings couldn't. Most of them were on a rampage, shouting, swearing, stealing each other's things. They may have had good reasons for feeling the way they did, but their jungle-like tactics only added to the already stressful conditions. The youngest, Jake, exercised the most self-control and seemed to be the most joyful. "I want to act mad, too," he said, "but I'm not going to."

Acknowledging one's anger is difficult. We all like to pretend that we don't feel it, that we're above such small emotion. Even if you don't admit it to yourself, your children see it. Abraham Lincoln once said, "I do not think much of a man who is not wiser today than he was yesterday." You are wiser in your children's eyes when you no longer take your frustrations out on your family.

When your son leaves a mess on the kitchen counter, be kind to him. When your daughter keeps talking even though you've asked her to get off the phone, ask her nicely again. Your children have circumstances that you don't know about. Being mature means rising above your knee-jerk reactions so that you can come to a deeper appreciation of your children's struggles.

 If you want to help your child manage his own anger, you have to be able to manage your own. Before you can help your angry child, you'll need to calm down yourself.

Recognize Warning Signs

From guns at school to neighborhood gangs, youth violence has become a hot topic. Yet if parents recognize the less sensational, more common types of aggression, perhaps we can prevent problematic acting out from becoming a habit. A little aggression, biting, pushing, grabbing, hitting, kicking is normal for a two-year-old; most will outgrow it as they learn social skills and acceptable behavior. A child who doesn't learn to control his impulses, however, becomes increasingly aggressive. By the time a child is seven or eight, you can start to recognize a pattern. Soon he's fighting in the schoolyard. Kids with other types of anger problems retreat, becoming more isolated, lonely, and hostile.

Following is a list of warning signs that your child is becoming violent:

1. Loses temper on a daily basis.

2. Frequently engages in physical fighting and vandalism.

3. Threatens to hurt others; hurts animals.

4. Is intrigued by guns and carries weapons.

5. Uses drugs and alcohol increasingly.

6. Has difficulty making friends or has unruly, aggressive friends.

7. Is isolated and lonely.

8. Doesn't express feelings.

The following factors may contribute to violence in children:

1. A parent who is violent and aggressive.

2. Presence of firearms in the house.

3. Drug and alcohol abuse by parents.

4. Exposure to verbal and physical abuse between the adults.

5. Physical and/or sexual abuse.

6. Repeated exposure to violent videos, movies, games.

7. Parents who condone or promote violence.

Persistent childhood aggression can become a lifelong issue. Adults who have problems with aggression demonstrated similar behaviors when they were children. Kids aren't born to hurt others; they learn it from the adults around them.

All these symptoms are cries for help. If you recognize these conditions in your family, please seek professional assistance. We all want to be appreciated and belong; your child wants that too. Don't turn your back and pretend you don't see that something's wrong. Don't convince yourself that it's not as bad as your gut feeling is telling you it is.

You won't be judged as a bad parent if you go for help, but you might be judged as a bad parent if you do nothing. Prevention is always better than punishment.

Use Talking Sticks

I like the idea of the talking stick that some cultures and groups use when discussing complaints, upsets, and concerns. I have two talking sticks that I use as reminders to my clients to pay close attention. One is a thick tree branch decoratively wrapped with leather straps. The other is a fluffy magic wand made of lace, beads, and glitter.

The talking stick is a tool of communication that makes talking about emotionally charged subjects more satisfying. Just holding the stick seems to gives the speaker the courage to say the truth and speak from the heart. The kid or parent who holds the stick has the floor until they've said all that they want to say. After the kids have finished, the parents might take a turn. As long as the person is holding the stick, no interrupting is allowed. The talking stick gives the speaker a chance to talk it all the way through, to speak of her true feelings, and to reveal what's beneath the surface.

Except for the socializing, fourteen-year-old Olivia says she hates school. She fights with her parents about homework and makes excuse after excuse about why she forgot to bring her books home, why she can't spell, why the teacher doesn't like her. It's always someone else's fault or the circumstances. "It was raining and I didn't want my books to get wet so I left them at school." Her parents are mad at her for not being responsible about her schoolwork, and she's angry at them for expecting her to be. The family talks about it, but they never really hear each other. The conversations take place in the middle of doing something else, on the run, or the participants interrupt each other.

Using the talking stick, Olivia talked about school and homework. At first she blamed the teachers, the desk, the stupid subjects that she'd knew she'll never need, her parents for bugging her, and on and on. She was plenty mad. As she continued to hold the talking stick, she talked more about what she was feeling, how unfair it was, how bored she was, and how afraid she was that she couldn't ever please her parents.

Most of what Olivia said was not new information. Olivia's parents had heard it before, but until that time in my office I don't think they had ever comprehended that Olivia was afraid that she could never please them. That was the beginning of a turnaround.

The talking stick is not magic. The magic happens through listening, hearing, listening, and hearing over and over again without threats or lambasting, without rebuttal or criticism. I don't like constructive criticism, either. When parents preference their remarks with "This is for your own good," children immediately brace themselves for something bad. Children respond best to options. When you give children choices, they're immediately less angry and more hopeful. They have a sense of power and a way to proceed.

Asking your child why he feels angry is a question of torture. Instead of asking "Why," say, "Help me understand." Then listen without interrupting, giving advice, freaking out, criticizing, butting in, or lecturing.

Take a Time Out, Take a Time In

Children need time to cool down. Talking in the heat of the moment only makes things hotter. Let your children know that it's OK to get mad and that after they've cooled down, you will talk about the matter with them. "I know you're mad that I grounded for the weekend. After you cool down, let's talk about it. Let's figure out how to avoid this next weekend."

Toddlers, preteens, teens, and parents can all benefit from time outs. A time out can be taken in a swing, on the floor next to a window, in a bedroom, or in a cozy corner. The purpose of a time out is not to punish the child for being angry. Its purpose is to teach the value of taking a break when you're mad. After a comforting time out, we all think more rationally and behave better.

Children need time for the fog to clear, time to rest and regroup. Young children frequently calm down when held on Mommy's lap. If you have exhausted all other warnings, you may need to hold young children who are oppositional and are refusing to take a time out until they can maintain a couple of minutes of quiet, calm sitting.

Preteens take longer to calm down. That's because they're fantasizing about how mean you are and how they're going to run away from home. Teens may laugh and sneer if you tell them to take a time out; if that happens you may have to restrict privileges to get their attention.

Just as your child needs a time out for cooling down, they also need a "time in" to talk about what happened. You'll want to hear their side of the story and what they learned; they need to hear your side and what you expect next time. A time out teaches a child the benefits of cooling off, impulse control, and how to delay gratification. When you send her off for a time out, tell her that you will have a time in with her when she's feeling relaxed and behaving, so that you can talk with her about what just happened.

 Follow a cooling-off time out with a time in to listen to your child's side of the story, to talk about what happened, and to teach skills for handling the situation in the future.

Pledge to Do No Harm

Parental anger hurts children. I worked for five years in a hospital emergency room in the Seattle area, and I have seen the results of parental anger. I've seen children with broken bones, black eyes, and welts—the results of punishment handed out by a raging parent. I've seen toddlers with hands burned by parents who said they were teaching the child the dangers of a touching a hot stove. I've seen infants with shaken baby syndrome, innocent victims who couldn't hold their heads up and were vomiting because they'd been shaken until their brains were damaged to the point of convulsions. I've seen the remorse and anguish of parents as they waited to find out if their child would live.

I tell you this because I don't ever want you to be waiting in a hospital emergency room while the child you injured is struggling for his life. I hope that you will recognize your frustration long before it ever gets to that point. Your children will get angry and so will you, but it's your responsibility to sense when you're on the verge of getting out of control.

When a parent refuses to take responsibility for her own anger, the relationship with her child is damaged. If you have an anger management problem, welcome feedback from others and go for counseling.

Every parent needs to sign this pledge:

"On my honor I pledge to do no harm to my children. I will not belittle my children or call them names. I will not shame them or abandon them. I will not physically abuse them. I will respect them as individuals. No matter what happens between me and my child's other parent, I will treat the other parent with respect and courtesy for the sake of my child. My child is a precious gift and I will always treat them as if God is watching. My children deserve to be treated with dignity. I will enjoy and see the world through their eyes. I will let them teach me."

 An immature parent knows she has an anger problem, but she doesn't do anything about it. A mature parent leaves no stone unturned in seeking help to overcome her angry, mean, cruel tendencies.

Stay Open to a Fresh Perspective

Peter and Clara, along with their eight-year-old son, Sam, and ten-year-old daughter, Katrina, sat in my office discussing the anguish the kids were experiencing over moving to another state. "You'll make lots of new friends, and the new house has a swimming pool," Clara said, trying to convince Sam and Katrina that the move would be fun. "We'll come back to visit Grandma and Grandpa in the summer and you can see your friends too," she added. Trying to cheer them up, Peter promised that they could talk on the phone and e-mail their friends. Then for the second time that hour, he launched into his story about his father being in the military and moving ten times as a kid. The kids weren't convinced. Sam slouched in the chair and jiggled his legs. Katrina stared out the window and twisted her hair. "This isn't easy for any of you," I said. Katrina burst into tears and Sam slouched further down into the chair. "What are you thinking?" I asked Sam. "Why can't we be mad?" he asked. Katrina wiped her tears and piped up, "Yeah! We're mad because we don't want to move. We know it will work out, but we want to be mad for awhile."

Kids are so smart. We've all felt that way—we know it will work out, but we want to be mad for a while. When things don't go according to our plans or don't work out exactly right, we feel frustrated. We know that eventually everything will be OK, but even though we know it, we're mad at first. Being mad is part of the adjustment. And as long as we're not hurting anyone, what harm can it do? In fact, allowing yourself to feel mad in the beginning, right when you first feel it, usually helps you feel better in the long run.

"That's a good suggestion," I said, and then I asked Peter and Clara if they could let Sam and Katrina be mad for awhile. I asked if maybe even Peter and Clara were mad. Then the funniest thing happened. Clara said that she was mad too, and she began listing the things about the move that made her mad. Sam cheered up immediately and joined in the game of listing the things that made him mad. Soon Katrina was adding to the list. As the three of them listed all the things that they were mad about, I noticed they were becoming quite lively and jolly. Sam was bouncing up and down and Katrina had moved closer to her mother. They were interrupting each other and laughing. "The cat's mad too because she doesn't know if there are birds in Arizona," Sam chuckled. I asked Peter if there was anything about the move that made him mad and he said he was mad because everyone else was mad. "So," he said, "I guess we're one big, happy, mad family." And they left the office smiling.

Funny, isn't it? Getting anger out in a non-hurtful way can often be an uplifting, energizing exercise. Feeling mad for a while and listing all the things that make you mad is often the beginning of making life OK.

 Allowing yourself and your children to feel mad when things go wrong is part of an adjustment that helps you all feel better in the long run.

PART 4 In the Presence of Colleagues

People are always blaming their circumstances for
what they are. I don't believe in circumstances. The
people who get on in this world are the people who
get up and look for the circumstances they want, and,
if they can't find them, make them.

—GEORGE BERNARD SHAW

When you master your anger, life on the job goes more smoothly. You
may have a boss who browbeats and bullies you, you may have a colleague who is prone to snide remarks and complaining, but you can
deal effectively with both of them. By fine-tuning your anger, you
empower yourself. Whether it's the sneaky, "This won't work" anger
of a negative team member, the agreeable yet nonproductive passive
anger of an employee, or the belligerent complaining of a client,
when you understand yourself, you can more easily manage the difficult people you encounter.

Managing does not mean getting along with them. You don't have
to like them, you don't have to change them, you don't have to invite
them to lunch. All you have to do is get the job done.

Dealing with an angry, boorish person is in some ways like dealing with the schoolyard bully. You want to get away from her as
quickly as possible, but if you're sharing an office cubicle that's often
not possible. What might be possible is to put distance between you
and the other person. You can do that by identifying what behavior
is driving you over the edge and then developing a strategy for

coping with that behavior. For example, an angry coworker might complain about even a minor mistake. Instead of getting defensive, which makes things worse, you might say, "I see what you mean," and leave it at that.

You can't change other people, but you can develop a procedure for dealing with troublesome behaviors. Focus on getting the job done. Focus on the task instead of the individual personality quirks, and you'll be less flustered and more detached.

Managing angry people requires that you act with intention and purpose. Instead of reacting in exasperation, you respond with deliberation and forethought. Instead of giving the angry person the power to make eight hours of your life miserable, you take back your power.

Difficult and angry people are everywhere. Even in the most compatible environment, there's usually someone who makes you angry. Their behavior is disruptive, frustrating, and counterproductive, but they don't see it. They unknowingly interfere with the business at hand. That's what makes working with them so unpleasant.

Learn Positive Self-Assertion

Self-assertion on the job is the ability to consciously choose between speaking up for yourself and being aggressive. Aggression is the compulsive, unconscious act of lashing out in order to hurt a coworker, to put her in her place, to squash her and put her down while making yourself feel better. Self-assertion, on the other hand, is taking action on your own behalf. It's being true to yourself with no intention to hurt others. Self-assertion focuses on making your own success. It's working hard, staying focused on the task, and getting the job done. It's being energetic, optimistic, and self-aware.

Most people become aware after they've "blown it." For example, you get angry at a coworker and talk behind his back. A customer gets angry, calls you nasty names, you snap back. After you've cooled down, you see how the situation quickly escalated. You understand what you could have done differently, but by then the damage has already been done. You can't take back your words or apologize enough.

To avoid the damaging consequences that anger on the job can bring, you need to develop awareness while the event, thoughts, and feelings are occurring. Anger can envelope you like thick smoke, and becoming aware of it while you're in the middle of the haze may be difficult at first, but it's definitely not impossible. With a little awareness you can catch hold of your anger before it encompasses you. You can become assertive instead of aggressive.

The first stage of awareness is noticing that you're angry and asking yourself, "What am I thinking at this moment?" The second stage is watching anger rise and fall as you notice what you're feeling, and the third stage is watching anger evaporate as you focus on your breathing. With awareness, you can watch anger swell, melt away, and vanish.

The next time you're angry at work, practice the three stages of awareness by saying to yourself:

1. "I'm angry. What am I thinking?"

2. "I'm watching anger rise and fall."

3. "I'm breathing in and out and anger is evaporating."

When you're angry, keep quiet. Don't speak up right away. Take a deep breath and notice how many minutes it takes for you to calm down. Anger awareness takes concentration at first, but it's truly worth the effort because the payoff is a more relaxed and powerful you; after a while awareness becomes part of your repertoire.

Angry people waste lots of time and energy on the job. They spout off about the unfairness of the boss, the system, the policies. They go on and on about how important they are or how others are messing up. They're caught up in thinking that if they had a different job, things would be better. Seldom do they see how they've contributed to their own self-defeating behaviors.

An assertive, successful person makes her own luck. When she's mad about something, she waits until she's decided what action to take. She thinks before she speaks. She does speak up, but she does it in such a way that she earns others' respect.

 When you're aware of what you are angry about you can choose to be assertive instead of aggressive.

Pay Attention to Your Needs

Anger on the job may be an indication that you've been neglecting yourself. Maybe you've been working so much overtime that you haven't had time to exercise, or perhaps you've been doing more than your share of the work. A client of mine who worked as a receptionist told me that she didn't take her morning break for three years because she worried about who would answer the phones while she was not at her desk. Then she started snapping at customers and got annoyed when her boss asked her a question. She figured out that she had worked for half an hour, five days a week, for three years, which added up to an additional $10,000 pay. No wonder she felt resentful.

If you've been paying attention to what others need while overlooking your own needs, mild anger is bound to surface, either through physical symptoms such as headaches or tight shoulders or through sarcastic comments. Eventually anger magnifies and infects your disposition. Maybe you've been neglecting to give yourself some much needed "do nothing" time.

We all have needs—physical and emotional—that need tending. If you're not taking care of yourself, you'll twist into a mean, unhappy grouch, and others will sense that in you. To avoid becoming known as the office sourpuss, do an inventory of yourself to make sure all your needs are met.

When we feel angry, our bodies are thrown into fight–flight mode. To relieve it we need to move, shake, or run. Paying attention to your bodily needs throughout the day prevents anxiety from building up. For example, if something angers you at work, going for a walk, pacing up and down the hallway, stretching at your desk will relieve the built-up tension in your body. Ask yourself these questions:

What does my body need?

Do I need to lie down or go for a walk?

Do I need to eat or drink something healthy?

Do I need to exercise on break?

Do I feel good in my clothes?

Are my shoes comfortable?

Do I need a massage during lunch hour?

Do I need to get my hair done? What about a manicure?

Work is not just about money, although being paid adequately is certainly important. In addition to good pay, we all need appreciation for our efforts, for showing up and contributing our best. Are you getting the appreciation and acknowledgment you want? Do you know that you are valued? Do you feel as if you're working with people you respect and trust? Are you spending enough time with friends and loved ones after work? What thoughts are you thinking at work? Are they uplifting or tearing you down?

The extra work Martha does at her entry-level position seldom is acknowledged, but she doesn't feel bitter because she's getting valuable experience and her foot in the door of her chosen field. She feels hurt sometimes and wishes for recognition, but she reminds herself of a personal goal—to complete the assignment for one year in order to gain the experience and contacts to move on. If the work that you're doing isn't appreciated, look for a way that you can adjust so that you don't feel taken advantage of.

 When you find yourself thinking angry, vengeful thoughts, stop and ask yourself, "What have I been neglecting? What do I need?"

Find Meaning in Your Work

Climbing the ladder of success can sometimes lead to loss of our souls. That's very dangerous, because when we lose our souls, darkness fills us and we become enraged and full of spite.

We all have a need to find meaning through our work. We long for work that matches our talents, that we enjoy, that we can pour our hearts into and believe in. We want to express our creativity. When we neglect our creative, talented selves we become stressed out and temperamental. The workday turns dreary and the future looks bleak. We become angry and bitter. You can't put in forty hours or more each week for fifty weeks a year at a job that you don't like and expect to live a life of contentment. If you start working when you're twenty years old at a job that isn't personally meaningful, and if you stay with it until you retire at sixty-five years old, that's forty-five years of resentment. Resentment at feeling trapped in a job takes a big toll on your overall well-being. Some people turn to greed and addictions to hide the growing ache. Others snap at loved ones the minute they walk through the door at the end of the day.

Have you been ignoring your desire for personally meaningful work? If you have work that allows for the expression of your creative nature, you are very fortunate. If your work doesn't allow for creative expression, you have a big challenge: either to find work that does, or to respond to your work situation in a creative way. Ask yourself:

Are the activities I do at work satisfying?

Is my work environment soothing?

Are conflicts resolved with compassion?

Am I working in accordance with my values?

Your work environment is important for your soul. What is the spirit of your workplace? Are your professional and personal values congruent? What are the workplace ethics? Do they match with yours? Compromising values for sake of a buck is harmful to your spirit.

We all have a sense of what we need to feel happy in our work, but often we focus on things that don't really satisfy—money, power, prestige—and when we do that we feel out of sorts and lose touch with our souls. If you find yourself chronically angry and resentful on the job, that may be a symptom of a lack of joy and meaning in your work. It's worth looking into.

It took Edward nine months of reflection to get up the nerve to resign from his high-tech management position. By asking himself the question, "What brings me joy in my work?" Edward discovered that money and stock options weren't enough. The most rewarding work for him was coaching basketball, which he was doing for free at the Boys Club. He went back to school and got a teaching certificate, and although he makes less money as a high school coach, he isn't mad any more. He finds joy and satisfaction in what he's doing.

If the mere thought of going to your job makes you uptight, anxious, cranky, or mad, then it's probably an indication that what you're doing at work doesn't match with your natural talents. If work doesn't add to your overall satisfaction with your life, then it's important to figure out what you'd rather be doing. Creating work that you enjoy washes away the resentments that build when you're dreading Monday morning and counting the hours until Friday. When you scan your workday, how much of what you do brings you joy and satisfaction? What would meaningful work be for you?

 You, dear friend, have the talent to make your work meaningful.

Lead with Gentleness

A gentle manner balances the force of anger in a powerful, effective way. When we think about anger, we usually think of harshness and violence. We don't have many role models that incorporate gentleness into the picture. A woman who can express her anger in a gentle way provides powerful leadership. She's usually a respected role model and a mentor. Colleagues trust her because they know she won't fly into a rage. Instead of blaming, she leads. She'll take responsibility; she doesn't take her anger out on others. She's direct and kindhearted. She's a motivating presence.

A man who uses anger to browbeat and conquer his coworkers is a scowling creature, but when he incorporates kindness and understanding he's respected as a wise and honorable leader whom others look up to and emulate. When you combine gentleness with whatever statements, demands, rules, or boundaries you set, associates and clients will respect you and cooperate.

To incorporate gentleness into your repertoire, it's imperative that you allow yourself to cool down when you feel angry. Before you blurt out demands or accusations, say something like, "Let's take a time out. I'm getting frustrated and I need to cool down." When we're angry we don't feel very gentle, and as a result we often lash out with a harshness or cruelty that hurts others and embarrasses us later.

When a colleague has a habit of coming to meetings late, you've been understanding, but after about the fifth time you're mad and want to talk with her about it. Remember: You can do it harshly or you can do it gently. You can be firm yet kind, powerful yet benevolent.

There's less tension in the air when you're gentle; confrontations are less dramatic and they don't last as long. When you balance anger with gentleness there's less strain and stress on your work relationship; you're more likely to stay connected than be torn apart.

When you're angry, waiting to calm down until you can be gentle is often the kindest action to take.

Respond

Some folks seem to think that anger, like a volcanic eruption, is beyond our control. At the first twinge of upset, they explode as if there were no other course. While they may momentarily feel vindicated, the end result is alienation from the people on the receiving end of the fallout. Anger always involves a *choice* between reacting and responding. You can choose whether or not to show your anger, how you want to express it, and who will be its focal point.

The difference between reacting and responding is significant. In the heat of the moment, all kinds of thoughts run through our minds. We're unable to think clearly. Our initial reaction is often based on false assumptions; acting hastily can make matters worse and have dire consequences for us. Responsibility is the ability to respond, and that takes discipline and maturity. You'll still feel the urgency of your impulses, but instead of allowing them to rule you, you choose what action to take and when to take it. Taking responsibility for your behavior means considering the consequences.

Joel's reaction, when he heard that the person just hired by his company was earning the same wages as he, was rage. He threw down his hammer, swore, walked off the job, and got drunk. Two days later, when the foreman called to find out why Joel was absent from work, Joel reacted again and told him where to go. It wasn't until a week later, when Joel went to pick up his check at the business office that he read the letter (that had been in his mail box since the previous month) announcing that he'd been given a raise. The only thing that all his storming and raging got him was "egg on his face."

This is just one example of what can happen when you freak out before you've gathered all the facts. When you're mad, instead of freaking out, gather the facts, then decide what to do. If you have a tendency to get mad and blow up, consider adopting this as your slogan: Finding out is more productive than freaking out!

 Wait twenty-four hours before responding to the person who provoked you. After you've investigated and gathered all the facts, then you can decide whether you want to respond, what response you want to make, and to whom you want to make it.

Use Neutral and De-escalating Language

If you work in a company that has a staff of more than one, you'll definitely need to perfect your anger management and negotiation skills. Temper tantrums don't get you very far up the ladder these days. Even if you have a tantrum-throwing boss, she probably won't like it if you do the same. At work you need to practice diplomacy. That means knowing when to speak up and when to keep quiet. You can't let anger run wild at work. You don't want to respond in ways that get others riled up. You will get miffed, and others will get annoyed with you, but you always have a choice as to what you do.

Many people get angry when you don't agree with them. Develop strategies to let bosses or colleagues know you disagree without alienating them.

Write the following sentences on a note card and paste them on your desk or at your computer. Take them to meetings, conferences, and lunch. Better yet, memorize each one. These sentences works best if you say them in an upbeat, friendly, lighthearted manner. Practice saying them out loud at home beforehand so that your voice is strong, confident, and friendly. In a heated situation, using these statements and questions will give you thinking time.

"I'm not sure what you mean. Could you explain that to me again?" or say, "Do you mean ... ?"

"I understand your point of view, but I don't have the same one. My point of view is different."

"I understand what you're saying, and I'd like time to think that over."

"I appreciate your approach, but my approach is different. You and I do things differently."

"Thank you for talking this over with me."

Whatever strategies you're developing, remember, good timing is critical in delivering the message. Don't confront an angry person in the middle of their outburst. Don't confront them when you're angry, either. Wait until you have both cooled down. Go over what you're going to say in your own mind first. If you need to talk about a potentially heated or emotionally charged topic, ask the person, "Can we schedule a short conference?" Angry, difficult people are super-sensitive to what others might be thinking. Talk to them in private and you'll avoid potential embarrassment.

Anger is a sign of a grievance that needs attention. You'll make more progress in solving the problem if you focus your attention on the grievance rather than on the person. If you're shouting at each other, neither of you is likely to get the results you're after. To really communicate, you have to be open to *not* knowing what to do. When you no longer have anything to say, then you can come to your colleague and address the work issue.

Using calm, neutral language can help two people who argue work successfully together.

Practice Good Manners

While I believe strongly in the value of expressing our opinions, I also believe strongly that there is a time and place for that expression. If everyone went around with their raw emotions pouring forth, the office would become filled with the tensions of the world. Dumping on and dissing colleagues and fellow team members at work is definitely self-defeating.

Good manners are good anger management tools. You can work out your grievances in a professional manner by incorporating these ten good manners on the job:

1. Conduct yourself in a way that reflects the good person that you are.

2. Be cordial to everyone regardless of their title or position.

3. Show your strengths in a positive way.

4. Accept help and assistance graciously.

5. Acknowledge the contributions of others.

6. Listen to other points of view.

7. Be respectful when you disagree.

8. State your opinions directly to the person involved.

9. When someone gives you a compliment, politely accept it by saying, "Thank you."

10. Expect good things to happen.

You determine how others perceive you. If you present an angry, gloomy persona, that's the impression others will have of you. To be successful on the job, put your emphasis on becoming the best that you can be. Polish your skills and let them shine. Set personal goals and focus on reaching them. Be pleasant about it.

 Good manners make ordinary life run more smoothly.

Watch Your Attitude

Tony, a young man I know, loves to cook. He trained as a chef, and upon graduation took a job cooking in an Italian bistro. He hated it. He said the problem was the boss. Tony got mad and quit. Then he took a position in a fish café. Guess what? Tony didn't like cooking fish. What was the problem? Was it the fish, the boss, or Tony's attitude? That's the puzzle we all face. What makes us hate our jobs? Is it the fish, the boss, or our own attitudes?

Everyone gets angry on the job, but unsuccessful workers get angry and blame it on others or on their circumstances. They're unhappy with their work and they know it, but since they need the money, they don't look at their issues directly. Instead they stifle, stall, avoid, and blame. Ineffectual workers put forth a minimal effort, they hold back. They won't admit mistakes, and when they do make one, instead of learning from it, they chew on that one little error for days. They won't accept help from others and think, "I'll do it myself." Unproductive workers are overly critical and won't listen to feedback. They engage in degrading remarks and negative thinking.

Successful people know their own strengths and weakness. They've identified their talents and have made a plan to obtain work that matches their skills and interests. They're winners because they focus on improving their own excellence. Instead of putting others down, they build everyone up. Winners inspire others to do their best. They support one another. They're able to make the best of whatever situation they face.

Each workday presents us with an opportunity to learn about ourselves. Winners in life take ordinary events as chances to investigate themselves further. If you're chronically angry at work, is the problem the work or is the problem inside of you? If you can't get along with the boss, is it you or is it her?

 A positive attitude is the bedrock of personal success.

Stick Up for Yourself

If you've ever had the adventure of crossing a canyon on a swinging rope bridge for the first time, you know the sense of accomplishment that comes when you finally arrive on the other side. Just as the rope bridge gets you from one side to the other, anger gets you to the other side of what's troubling you. Learning to speak up when you're mad about something at work is like walking a rope bridge: it gets your adrenaline pumping. And it requires similar skills: spunk, concentration, and perseverance. You step out, you're unstable, it feels precarious. You want to run, to freeze, to turn back, but you don't. You've made up your mind: you'll put one foot in front of the other until you reach the other side. When you finally land safely on solid ground, you look back, breathe a sigh of relief, and say to yourself, "That wasn't so bad."

Expressing yourself clearly at work is an art worth learning. Whether it's dealing with an angry customer, an ill-tempered boss, an unfair personnel practice, you'll need to speak up or on your own behalf. We all spend so much time working that unless we can speak up, we feel taken advantage of, and then our attitude can quickly turn sour. Speaking up makes work more enjoyable. You feel connected, involved.

You're mad about something! You don't like what's been going on, so this time you're determined to make a change. You persevere, you repeat yourself, you stop, and in a split second you're speaking out again. You're not backing down; you won't give up. You make your point. You took a chance, and nothing bad happened. You shoulders relax. The anger didn't last long; in fact it's gone.

The human spirit is amazing. It has created great works of art, it has overthrown tyrannies, it has overcome tremendous obstacles. You have that self-same beautiful human spirit. You have unique abilities. What the mirror tells you is not terribly important. When you look into your mirror, instead of looking for blemishes, look for your soul. Look for the intelligent creative child, because that child is still there inside you and always will be—regardless of how many mistakes you may have made, regardless of how angry you feel now.

Love yourself! Love yourself for doing the best you can. Recognize that although things were not always easy for you, you've still done a lot of good things. Love yourself as much as you can. If you do that, creativity will express itself in your work.

One of the best ways of loving yourself is by sticking up for yourself. Above all, stick up for yourself in the tussles at work, because otherwise you will dread going in. The more you stick up for yourself, the more you will appreciate yourself and the contribution you make.

 Standing up for yourself by speaking out is more productive and invigorating than being manipulative.

Be Determined

People who turn anger into determination develop self-assurance. They become a powerful presence with poise and aplomb.

After an acrid divorce, Victoria was sick and tired of being the victim of her ex's authoritarian know-it-all attitude. Not wanting to turn into a bitter women, she knew she'd need to turn her "get even" energy toward building a good life for herself instead of griping about what a raw deal she'd gotten in the divorce.

Returning to work after fifteen years and without a formal education, she knew she couldn't start at management level. Yet the thought of having a subordinate position left her feeling cranky. Considering her temperament, she said, "I need a job with some power." Then she brainstormed with friends and advisors: "What kind of a job can I find where my cranky stubborn disposition might be beneficial?"

After a lengthy process of trial and error, career counseling, and twenty-plus interviews, Victoria landed a job as a collection agent. She turned her crankiness into firmness, and although she was never nasty to the public, she was steadfast. She rose to management level quickly. Instead of being bitter and trying to get even with her ex-husband, she turned her anger into a successful career. She decided, as you probably have, too, that living a good life is the best revenge.

Many people have used their angry energy to accomplish great things. The founder of Mothers Against Drunk Driving turned her grief and anger into an organization to educate the public about drinking and driving. We all have plenty of things to rile us up. Let's make a pact with one another to use our anger and energy to get things done.

 Great things can happen when you channel your anger into creating positive change.

Clarify the Conflict

It's often confusing to determine who is responsible for what. In the workplace, that often leads to conflict. Letting the other person know that you want to continue to improve your working relationship is the beginning of conflict resolution. Saying, "Let's deal together with our conflict" sets the tone for a positive outcome. Choose a conducive time, a nonthreatening corner of the office, and close the door. Begin by saying, "By working this through now, we can improve the way we handle problems that might arise in the future." Then add, "You and I are partners in this conflict, and I'm looking forward to working it out."

Clarifying both parties' perceptions of the conflict is a big part of the process. Ask yourself, "What is the conflict about for me? Is this conflict about one issue or does it reveal deeper problems in the office?" Ask your partner, "What is the conflict or problem as you see it?" Listen to what they're saying, and if you don't understand ask them to clarify again by saying, "Do you mean...?" Make sure you understand what's troubling your colleague before you move on. Help your colleague to clarify his thoughts, don't force him to defend them.

The time you put into clarifying the issues up front will save you trouble on the other end. Conflicts have a past, a present, and a future. To clear it up you have to tackle all three. By clarifying what happened in the past, you can understand the present conflict and make adjustments to prevent it in the future. Clarifying is an ongoing process. No need to rush or be defensive.

 Clarifying the conflict is the first step in finding a solution.

Don't Be Outraged, Be Outrageous

If you're shocked by the injustice around you or by the wrongs inflicted upon you, instead of being outraged, be outrageous. Look around and you'll notice how foolish others are when they're trying to seek revenge. Ranting, raving, settling scores, power plays, and scheming are common these days, but they are weak and mediocre reactions.

Dare to make a quantum leap. Become a leader, a positive role model, an exceptional person. Anger, as a refined emotion, can mend a broken heart, heal a family, unite a community, and excite a nation. Anger can motivate you to make big strides toward innovation.

Remember, freedom is the ability to respond to every situation in a new way. If you don't like your job but can't quit, if you like the pay but don't like the hours, if you have an idea for a way to simplify procedures, then do something about it. Instead of moaning and groaning about what seems impossible, shift your focus and make it possible.

Many years ago I was burned out from my full-time job as a social worker on the night shift in a hospital emergency room. I needed the job, but I could no longer manage all the hours, and my attitude was turning cranky. I mentioned my desire for fewer hours to a colleague and discovered she too wanted fewer hours. Our supervisor said it was impossible to cut our hours. We were discouraged but stubborn. We persevered and did our homework. One month later, with carefully researched documentation in hand, we made an oral and written presentation outlining the benefits to the hospital of job sharing. Three months later we were the first employees at Steven's Hospital to share a job. Not only did our proposal work for us personally, but as a result the board of directors extended hospital benefits to all employees working twenty hours per week.

We all have the power to turn frustration into innovation. A client of mine proposed telecommuting to her company. She now works from her home two days each week. Another company, at the suggestion of an employee, implemented movie Fridays. A public relations company, as a result of an employee's suggestion, conducts their employment interviews at the coffee shop in the building.

Be the best at what you are doing. Find one thing that you like about your work and focus on that. Get involved in changing policies; find ways to make your work life flexible and fun. If someone hurts you, don't waste your strengths fighting with them. If you want to fight—find a cause and fight for that. Assemble your talents and do something about the larger injustices. Trust your strengths and use them to become a leader, a champion for others to follow. Experiment with going into difficult conflict-like situations, and see what you can accomplish. Instead of avoiding conflict by retreating to where things are agreed upon in advance, go out where it's really difficult and practice healing negotiation.

 Respond to injustice by using your outrage as a force for change.

Stay with the Discomfort

It's in the trenches of bumbling along that you learn about yourself and about how you handle conflict. It's not from theories; it's in limping along through workday strife that you learn about the nuances of anger and how to face the opposition. You blow up even though you promised yourself that you wouldn't. Instead of stating your case clearly, you cry and are convinced you've made a fool of yourself. You want to understand the reasons that your two colleagues are ignoring you, but you feel rejected. Learning to deal with anger isn't easy.

A team member on the fund raising-committee told Ellen that the way she was organizing the campaign was not efficient. Ellen was shocked by the comment, but instead of asking for clarification, she ran out of the room in tears. "I couldn't think straight," she said later. "I've been doing extra work, but maybe I just don't understand what they want. I wish I could speak up without crying," Ellen said. "I don't want to be on the committee anymore." Ellen doesn't want to cause waves or make trouble, so instead of staying with her discomfort and asking for clarification, she withdraws. She wants to assert her viewpoint, but she puts on a hurt demeanor and convinces herself, that "it doesn't matter." But she pays a high price. She ends up feeling misunderstood and isolated. She gives up.

It's fun to be part of a group of people pulling together for the same goal. When the progress goes smoothly we enjoy it, but as soon as there is a little glitch we wonder if it's worth the hassle. But if you drop out every time the going gets rough, you never attain the victory that comes with accomplishment.

There's victory in conquering your reticence about conflict. There's triumph in hanging in there and sorting it out. You have a valuable contribution to make, and even if others don't always agree, you can listen to what they have to say and see if you can benefit from it. Then you can state your point of view, because after all you might present things from an angle that was never considered till you spoke up.

 Working your way through your discomfort with conflict can reap huge benefits in your confidence and in the contributions you can make.

Get Over Road Rage

I've changed quite a few of the patterns in my life. I don't let people take advantage of my good nature to the point that I feel walked upon, I speak up about issues that are important to me, and I let small stuff slide. One absolute rule I've adopted is, Be watchful behind the wheel.

You've noticed how egotistical people behave when they're behind the wheel: tailgating, cutting people off, racing, demanding their spot on the road, honking, cussing and cursing as if they're the only ones who know how driving should be done. Road ragers take their aggressions out on innocent drivers; they use their cars as weapons.

My client Mark had an attack of road rage and purposely rammed his car into a van that had cut him off for a parking space. For a brief moment, Mark felt vindicated, but when he saw that the driver was a young mother with a baby in the back seat, he felt like a complete nincompoop. Most of the time Mark's a mellow guy, but behind the wheel the Rambo side of his personality emerges. To change his automatic rageful reactions, he had to practice conscious defensive driving. Not only did he have to abide by the rules of the road, he had to pay attention to his mood and remain unflappable— he had to wake up and not be overtaken by his vengeful urges.

Buddhists engage in a spiritual practice called "mindfulness." It's a quality of being attentive to what is happening inside of you— in your thoughts and your feelings, in your body and mind. Mindfulness frees us from the conditioned responses that restrict our ability to see the world objectively. Paying attention to your conditioned reactions when you're behind the wheel is helpful in conquering road rage.

Before getting behind the wheel, take a moment to remind yourself that you can feel good when you're driving. You can't control the pace of the traffic, congestion, other drivers, or road conditions, but you can control your own attitude. You can stay peaceful and centered, confident in your ability to get where you're going. When stuck in a traffic jam, you can freak out and work yourself up to a frenzy, or you can shift to an "easy does it" rhythm. When you're cut off, you can become agitated, or you can say to yourself, "Oh well," and practice nonaggression. Content behind the wheel, you'll get to where you're going with a pleasant disposition. Victor Frankel, author of *Man's Search for Meaning,* was in several Nazi death camps and survived. He later wrote, "The last human freedom is the ability to choose one's attitude. We have some of the divine in us. We can turn misery into joy, hate into love, anger into forgiveness."

 You can enjoy a trip in your car or the drive to work by focusing on your surroundings—the houses, the trees, the colors. Instead of being passive and in a daze, you'll be awake and attentive.

Identify Your Hot Buttons

Hot buttons are those pesky little triggers that drive you over the edge. Lois had a pattern of quitting one job after another, because something always made her mad. Before she identified her hot buttons, she thought getting mad went with being in the workforce. Lois tried to avoid conflict, she tried to get along, but sooner or later a coworker would say something that she didn't like, and she'd hand in her resignation. Then Lois got the design job of her dreams, with good pay and creative responsibilities. She adored the work; it made her heart sing. Everything was going smoothly until a new employee was hired. Right off the bat, Lois couldn't stand her, and in her own mind she started to build a case against the coworker. Now Lois was stuck. She didn't want to quit, but she couldn't do her job feeling mad every moment. Lois wished the other person would go away, but since that wasn't likely, she decided to figure out if there was a lesson she needed to learn.

With the assistance of a career coach, Lois uncovered what triggered her anger. Whenever her coworker was acknowledged for doing a good job, Lois felt jealous. Her boss appreciated Lois' work and showed it often, but still Lois felt competitive. To get over getting mad at work, Lois had to stop comparing herself to others. Comparing yourself is always painful; it breeds anger and resentment. With the new realization, Lois made a shift; she stopped competing and put her energy into doing a fabulous job.

Meg landed her first big catering account and stumbled onto one of her hot buttons. She'd hired several friends to serve at an afternoon garden party and told them to wear black. When one of them showed up in black shorts, Meg was fuming. Having a professional image is important to her, and since not everyone agrees on what that might be, Meg designed a company uniform—blue dress, white apron. Now she has one less thing to get crazed about.

 Identifying your hot buttons is good preventative anger management. When you know your hot buttons, you can take measures to unplug them before seeing red.

Give Yourself Breathing Space

If you've ever been called on the carpet by a boss whom you thought was a jerk, if you've ever worked with a team of folks with whom you weren't compatible, if you've handled complaints from distraught customers, then you know what a challenge it can be to tackle issues without getting defensive and tongue-tied.

Joan was called into her bosses' office for an unexpected conference. The boss explained that two team members had complained that Joan was sloughing off. The boss had noticed that Joan had lost her enthusiasm for the project and was wondering what the issues were. Joan turned red in the face and became defensive. She was mad! Instead of saying, "I'd like to think over your concerns and get back to you," which would have given her some breathing space and thinking time, she blurted out double talk, excuses, and accusations. "That's not true," and "We have too much work to do," and "They don't like me" only made matters worse.

There are countless work situations where you'll need to give yourself some breathing space. A boss who makes unreasonable demands, a client's dissatisfaction, a colleague who doesn't see it your way. That's when you need breathing space to clarify your strategy. Breathing deeply works in all kinds of tense situations. If you get in the practice of breathing deeply, you can use the technique to avoid saying nasty things. When you're mad or defensive, take five deep breaths—exhale, inhale—and see where your anger goes. Breathing helps you relax, and you can do it at your desk.

With some breathing space, you can begin to clarify what is troubling you. With breathing space, you can identify your concerns, upsets, disagreements, or annoyances and choose an effective strategy for tackling the situation.

When something is troubling you, take breathing space at your desk and answer these questions:

What is my upset, concern, or disagreement? (Be specific.)

Who is the person or persons I must talk with to resolve this issue?

What am I asking the person to do so that this issue can be resolved? (Be specific.)

What am I willing to do to solve this matter? (Be specific.)

To right a wrong, you don't have to get angry. How many times did your lashing out only make things worse? Acting in anger is often worse than not acting at all. Regardless of how many mistakes you may have made, respect yourself for doing the best you can. Recognize that although things were not always easy for you, you've still done a lot of good things.

 When you're upset with a colleague, give yourself breathing space by saying, "I'd like to think that over and get back to you." Breathe, develop a strategy, and then go back to your colleague and clear it up.

Spread Heavenly Gossip

Everyone gossips, but not everyone is conscientious about it. There are two kinds of gossip—hurtful and heavenly—and if you've lived past the age of seven, you've probably participated in both kinds.

There's hurtful gossip that originates in jealousy. Perhaps you've told or listened to a disparaging story about someone else that was really none of your business. You came away with a gnawing sense of superiority and smugness. We've all passed on a piece of gossip that was hurtful because we distorted the facts to make ourselves look innocent. We've all said something we were sorry for the minute it came out of our mouth. Destructive gossip gets stale, gives you a headache, a stomachache, and pulls your energy down. On many contemporary talk shows, guests are encouraged to bare their souls, yet the audience turns on them and uses the information shared to put the person down. It's the modern version of throwing the Christians to the lions.

Heavenly gossip is much more joyful than destructive gossip. Heavenly gossip, like fine poetry or a vibrant symphony, nourishes your soul.

What is heavenly gossip? It is a story that tugs at your heart, gives you goosebumps, puts a lump in your throat, or makes you laugh till you fall down. Heavenly gossip has a shocking quality about it; it wakes you up, it comes from truth. The person sharing it is vulnerable, revealing him- or herself openly, honestly, purely. It comes simply. It's clean, with nothing to hide.

To understand heavenly gossip, you need to have sensitive ears and a very sympathetic heart. When you listen to the stories, your inner light shines, the darkness disappears, and you're alive and dancing. Jesus, Buddha, Lao Tzu told their stories in a very poetic way, filled with metaphors. Their stories were beyond fact and fiction, yet centuries later they still penetrate our hearts, and we know we've heard the Truth.

Heavenly gossip is a way of saying things that cannot be said. It is not meant strictly for your entertainment; heavenly gossip transforms. Heavenly gossip has a message in it, and you'll have to listen closely to find it.

Your own approach to gossip is important. Judging a story or a person is not important. If a story lifts you up, soak it in and share it with another; if you learn something about the dark side of yourself, rejoice. If a story pulls you down, leave it. If don't want to hang out in sleaze, if you're not interested in slander, defamation of character, or rumor, give up tabloids and contrived talk shows. Don't watch violence. Develop the knack of spreading heavenly gossip.

Heavenly gossip, like great poetry, should lift you up. It's the only kind of gossip to spread.

RESOURCE GUIDE

For a listing of anger management classes in your community,
call a local hospital or mental health clinic.

Associations and Organizations

Abused Men Association
www.abusedmen.org

The American Coalition for Fathers and Children
www.acfc.org

Center for Media Literacy
1962 South Shenandoah
Los Angeles, CA 90034
899-226-9494

Center to Prevent Handgun Violence
1225 Eye Street NW, Suite 1100
Washington, DC 20005
202-289-7319
www.handguncontrol.org

Community for Creative Non-Violence
425 2nd Street NW
Washington, DC 20001
202-393-1909
www.erols.com/ccnv

Domestic Violence Centers, by State
www.sboard.org/shelters.html

Foundation for the Prevention of Child Abuse
3050 Central Avenue
Toledo, OH 43606-1700
419-535-1989
www.preventchildabuse.com

Educators for Social Responsibility
23 Garden Street
Cambridge, MA 02138
www.esmational.org

Institute for Mental Health Initiatives
Channeling Children's Anger
4545 42nd Street NW, Suite 311
Washington, DC 20016
202-364-7111
www.imhi.org

The National Domestic Violence Hotline
800-799-7233
www.ndvh.org

National Resource Center on Domestic Violence
800-537-2238

National Youth Crisis Hotline
800-448-4663

Peace Education International
Award-winning materials for teaching children the skills of nonviolent conflict resolution.
888-667-3223
www.kidspeacenet.com

Women Helping Battered Women
800-228-7395

Women's Rape Crisis Center
800-489-7273

Books on Anger

Anger: How to Live With and Without It, by Albert Ellis (Secaucus, N.J.: Carol Publishing Group, 1977).

Anger: The Misunderstood Emotion, by Carol Travis (New York: Simon and Schuster, 1989).

The Anger Book, by Theodore Rubin (Macmillan, 1969).

The Dance of Anger, by Harriet Lerner (New York: Harper & Row, 1985).

The Defiant Child: A Parent's Guide to Oppositional Defiant Disorder, by Dr. Douglas A. Riley (Dallas, TX: Taylor Publishing, 1997).

How to Express Anger (Without Hurting Yourself or Others) To order this pamphlet for your school or organization call: Journeyworks Publishing, 800-775-1998.

150 Facts about Grieving Children, by Erin Linn (San Francisco, CA: Mark Publishing, 1990).

When Anger Hurts Your Kids: A Parents' Guide, by Matthew McKay, Ph.D., and Patrick Fanning (Oakland, CA: New Harbinger, 1996).

Web Sites

Family Information
www.familyeducation.com
www.parentsoup.com
www.parents.com

Overcoming Abusive Relationships
www.cybergirl.com
www.emergedy.com
www.pavnet.org

Self-Assessment
Although these are not scientific, you can take these self-assessment tests online and identify your tendencies.

Identify Your Personality Type
www.keirsey.com

Parenting with Love and Laughter Quiz
www.judyford.com
/jfparentingquiz.html

Road Rage
www.queendom.com
www.drivers.com

Stress Test
www.eap.com.au/
stress_test.htm>

Supersensitive Person Test
www.supersensitiveperson.com/sel
ftest2.html>

A Wide Collection of Self-Assessment Tests
www.acc.scu.edu/~tnahal/
psych.html>

Women Watch
www.un.org/womenwatch/

Music to Open Your Heart

Amazing Grace, Mahalia Jackson

Amazing Grace: The Inspirational Collection, B. J. Thomas

Songs from a Parent to a Child,
Art Garfunkel
Be sure to listen to "Good Luck Charm," a duet with son James.

Other

To order Sprinkles:
www.livelovelaugh.com

ACKNOWLEDGMENTS

This book came to be because my mentor and dearest friend, William Ashoka Ross, believed in me and loved me enough to let me get mad. Mary Jane Ryan of Conari Press kept the concept alive for five years while teaching me how to write. Leslie Berriman, my optimistic editor at Conari Press, and Pam Suwinsky, copyeditor, brilliantly smoothed out the manuscript. Brenda Knight, sales director, continues to encourage my work by selling thousands of my books.

Tad Benson, Cliff Durfee, Bob Edwards, Marie Guise, M.A., Julie Hotard, Ph.D., Virginia Kimball, Chloe Patton, Cathy Schalkle, and Jean Theisen contributed much appreciated life experience, handholding, and chocolate. Jay Schlechter, Ph.D., whose sweet laughter softens my heart, shared his wisdom and called every day to check on me and keep me going.

Other Books By The Author

Wonderful Ways to Love a Child

Wonderful Ways to Love a Teenager

Wonderful Ways to Be a Family

Wonderful Ways to Be a Stepparent

Wonderful Ways to Love a Grandchild

Blessed Expectations

Between Mother and Daughter

ABOUT THE AUTHOR

Judy Ford, L.C.S.W., a nationally recognized family therapist, educator, and bestselling author, has dedicated her life to family healing and wholeness. She has worked for nearly three decades with children and families in various settings—from gang turf in the inner city to crisis intervention in hospitals. Her anger management workshops, "Winning Ways to Handle Conflicts, Complaints, and Little Annoyances" have been attended by thousands. A family therapist, she resides in Washington state with her daughter.

Workshop and speaking information is
available at Judy's Web site: www.judyford.com

or you may write:

Judy Ford, L.C.S.W.
P. O. Box 834
Kirkland, WA 98083
or e-mail:
judy@judyford.com

TO OUR READERS

Conari Press publishes books on topics ranging from spirituality, personal growth, and relationships to women's issues, parenting, and social issues. Our mission is to publish quality books that will make a difference in people's lives—how we feel about ourselves and how we relate to one another. We value integrity, compassion, and receptivity, both in the books we publish and in the way we do business.

As a member of the community, we sponsor the Random Acts of Kindness™ Foundation, the guiding force behind Random Acts of Kindness™ Week. We donate our damaged books to nonprofit organizations, dedicate a portion of our proceeds from certain books to charitable causes, and continually look for new ways to use natural resources as wisely as possible.

Our readers are our most important resource, and we value your input, suggestions, and ideas about what you would like to see published. Please feel free to contact us, to request our latest book catalog, or to be added to our mailing list.

2550 Ninth Street, Suite 101
Berkeley, California 94710-2551
800-685-9595 • 510-649-7175
fax: 510-649-7190
e-mail: conari@conari.com
www.conari.com